GOING DOWN IN GOTHAM

ZOE HANSEN

www.farwestpress.com

First Edition

ISBN 979-8-9943356-2-8

Printed in the United States of America

Cover Artwork by Olya Dyer

For Jerry and Jake

CONTENTS

THE ROBBERY

"Character—the willingness to accept responsibility for one's own life—is the source from which self-respect springs." — Joan Didion

Something terrible had just gone down. The call came from one of my security guards: get down to Sterling Ladies immediately. My cab pulled up to 21st Street and Park Avenue just as the rain stopped. Below on the sidewalk, couples laughed, picking up last-minute groceries for Thanksgiving dinner. They had no idea what horror waited upstairs.

I took the stairs two at a time, heart hammering. One deep breath, then I opened the door.

Max let me in, his face ghost white. Every overhead light blazed, illuminating the chaos and my traumatized employees scattered around the trashed apartment.

"What the hell just happened?"

Max hung his head. "They put Louie and me in the bathroom and stripped us naked. Made us kneel with our hands zip-tied behind us." His voice cracked. "Can you believe this shit? We were robbed."

The words hit me like ice water. My beautiful brothel. My people, all my hard work.

"Zoe, they put pillowcases over our heads!" Max continued; his usual FM-DJ coolness completely gone. "I thought we were gonna die, right there on that spot."

His pouty lips tried to form a grin, but it came out crooked. "Are you sure this isn't the afterlife? Am I dead?"

I wrapped my arms around his slender shoulders, feeling him shake.

This is the thing about my world: everything is

rolling along just fine, business can be fantastic one minute, then turn to pure hell the next. Sterling Ladies had been booming, but in this game, success makes you a target.

"They had nine-millimeters," Max went on, wiping a tear from his cheek. "Semi-automatics with homemade silencers. They looked real, very real, and I don't know shit about guns."

"So how the fuck did they get in?"

Max caught my eye, guilt written all over his face. "I went to do laundry. Left the door on the latch. I know, I know. But I could see the front door. I do it all the time, never take my eyes off it. Zoe, I'm so sorry."

I couldn't blame him. Max was my right-hand man, the person I trusted most in this business. It was a simple mistake, the kind anyone could make. But in my world, one simple mistake can cost you everything.

"Zoe, they took my mom's wallet," Mercedes sniffled from the couch. "The one she gave me before she died."

"Oh honey, I'm so sorry." But even as I comforted her, my brain was already doing the math. If the landlord found out, and he would, we'd have to relocate.

Ten grand minimum.

Finding the right place wasn't just about money. I needed somewhere without a doorman, somewhere that would turn a blind eye to my illegal business.

"Who did it?" I asked, looking around at my destroyed apartment.

One face kept surfacing in my mind: that woman. I'd been warned not to hire her, but I was desperate and ignored my gut. Stupid.

"They made us strip naked," Mercedes continued. "It was so embarrassing. And I had a client here. My regular, Alan. They really fucked with him, and stole his Rolex, you know the one Ozzy apparently gave him, then they shoved him in the closet."

We all stared at the open closet door, clothes spilling out like guts.

"I thought they were going to rape us," Desire said through her tears. "Then they hogtied us, those pieces of shit, coward motherfuckers."

"Ay dios mio, they took the jewelry right out of our ears." Desire's voice broke. "My little studs from my Nonie. They took my grandma's earrings! Los bastardos!"

"Oh no, Jamie lent me her fur jacket!" another girl wailed. "They took her fur! What am I gonna do, Zoe? She's gonna kill me."

"Does anyone know what they looked like?"

"Two guys with masks," Max said. "But they were definitely black, big guys. Like massive, intimidating bouncers."

"They went through everything," Mercedes added, her voice shaking. "Took our IDs. Said they would come to our houses. I have kids, Zoe."

"I promise you, they aren't going to show up at your house," I said, trying to sound more confident than I felt. "They're just trying to scare you."

But honestly? I had no clue if they'd follow through. The terror was the whole point.

We sat in the destroyed living room like survivors of a bombing, going through every woman on the schedule. Was it this one? Was it her?

Why should I be shocked? These are criminals, all of us. My life has no security net, no steady paycheck, no normal anything. This is the path I chose.

That's when Max delivered the final blow.

"Zoe, they got the safe."

Silence. Complete, crushing silence. I held my breath as a chill ran down my spine. I'd been so busy with day-to-day operations that I'd forgotten to take the week's drop home. Of course, they came for the safe.

"I'm tired as fuck," Nicole said finally. "I gotta go home. What are we gonna do?"

I looked at her, this tough woman who'd just lived through hell. "Are we not working girls?" I said with a smile that felt foreign on my face. "Are we not professional women? Nothing stops a hoe. We run the universe, don't we?"

I hugged her tight. "If you're willing, I'm going to open up. See you at ten?"

"I'll be here," she said, hugging me back. "Nicole," I said, the lump in my throat making

my voice rough. "I just want you to know I love and appreciate you. We will get through this."

After everyone else left, Max and I stayed behind, trying to put the pieces back together. We work with hard women, all of us damaged in our own ways. Anger always simmers just below the surface. Some will say "snitches get stitches" one day, then call the cops the next.

In this business, nothing ever goes smoothly. And this? This was just the beginning.

COPS AND DEAD BODIES

*"Every woman in the world is a whore; some just have
to work harder for their money than others."*
— *Anaïs Nin, Little Birds*

Three days after the robbery, I stood across the street from my building watching two police cars idle in front of the entrance.

From a block away, the emergency vehicles were parked on an otherwise empty Park Avenue South. Fear and blinding panic settled in my gut.

The police vehicles can't be for us. Surely not. Can they?

I stumbled out of the cab and called Max from a corner payphone with trembling fingers. "M-M-Max," I stammered. "What the fuck? There are two emergency vehicles in front of our building! Tell me it's not for us. Please God, no."

"And good morning to you, Zoe, how are you?" Max purred.

"You're not gonna believe this," Max started, his voice dropping to a whisper. "The cops are here. Apparently, someone called 911 and said there was a dead body up here."

"What?" I shrieked into the payphone. "Why are you talking about a dead body? Who the hell is it?"

Who do you call when a dead body appears in your brothel?

"They didn't ask who owned the place, did they?" I braced for whatever fresh hell was about to unfold.

"Well, they did, but of course I told them I didn't know. None of the women said anything about you." Thank goodness for small miracles, and my loyal employees.

I was looking at twenty years for promoting and

pandering if they connected me to the apartment.

I'd taken steps to avoid any connection between this apartment and myself. But my employees didn't know that, and might talk if it meant getting out of trouble. So far, no one seemed to have mentioned that I was the owner.

"Not sure who the body is," Max continued, "because, you know, they can't find a body. There isn't any dead body up here. It must be Princess. She called it in to fuck us up again, ruin business."

Princess. Of course.

Standing on the ancient church steps across the street, I watched the team of cops move back and forth between their vehicles and my building like worker ants dismantling a hill.

I'd been desperate for a replacement after discovering that a "friend" I'd hired to answer my phones had stolen a substantial amount of my money. Funds I needed for bills and rent. The same "friend" I'd just bought a round-trip ticket to visit some guy in Colombia. It was an outrageous betrayal.

Princess had arrived through someone from another house. Dark-skinned and significantly overweight, she wore no makeup and kept her hair cropped short. But it was her unsettling, fixed sneer that truly disturbed me. Princess never quite met my gaze, and when she did, her eyes held something deeply unsettling. But I hired her anyway. Hiring someone without a thorough background check is the kind of questionable decision you make when you're completely backed into a corner.

Then she started selling ecstasy to the women. Having recently quit drinking and drugs myself, I'd established a strict drug-free policy at work. But one day I arrived at the office at noon and found five of the women high as hell, drifting around in that god-awful "I love you and everything around me" ecstasy stupor. They were forgetting to charge and collect tips and were likely doing way more in the room than necessary, which ruined good clients for the rest of us.

I warned her. She promised she'd stop. She didn't stop.

So I fired her.

And she looked at me with pure hatred and said, "You'll regret this."

I should have seen it coming.

After what felt like hours, the cops finally drove off. I waited, then called Max.

"So, are they gone?"

"Yep," he replied, relief evident in his voice. "Come on up, honey."

I tore across the street and up the back stairs, heart hammering. Inside, Max threw his hands up at the destruction. "Jesus, look at this mess. Was this really necessary? It's excessive."

Black soot covered our walls like storm clouds. "Because they fingerprinted everything," Mercedes said, pointing to the smudged powder. "Even the walls. You're gonna have to repaint."

"Repaint my ass," Max muttered, peering at a smudged handprint.

I slumped down at the desk, utterly defeated. All my hard work, gone. "What an insane mess. And a dead body? Come on. I think the cops are fucking with us."

"Max, you know what this means, right? We have to move. It's done, over."

My gorgeous whorehouse, on this perfect block with the coolest staff. We'd had a good run, a whole year, and built a solid list of regulars.

But I would not give up.

I'd been here before. Burned, betrayed, starting from zero. At just 16 years old I was thrown out of my house by my father at 11 PM. That night he drove me to my heroin dealer's house. I moved to New York City at 17 years old. And I've been finding my way ever since. With no direction or help, I've had to navigate this world alone, adding and detracting members to my collective family along the way. There is no course for how to stay alive and sane living in the underworld. It's a lesson you either get or pass. I got it and have been honing my talents. I'm not suggesting I had no alternative to prostitution. Of course I could have. I chose this life and profession, and I wanted to be a really good madam. I wanted to give my employees a safe, enjoyable place where we could all benefit mutually.

The worst part about betrayal isn't the moment it happens. It's the aftermath, when you're left standing in the wreckage trying to figure out how to keep breathing.

But here's what Princess didn't know about me: Even though she saw a young woman of certain privilege, I'd come up hard. No amount of private boarding schools and British façade of upper middle class could take away that I was and have always been on my own. Everything I had was gained from street smarts and illegal activities. I had dealt with diabolical females forever. My mother was one, and I'd been taking notes.

I gave myself twenty-four hours to find a new place in which we could continue business uninterrupted. And I gave myself one promise: the next time someone came for me, I'd see them coming.

TRAINING FOR PROFESSIONAL SEX WORK

"I like freedom. You can't get any freedom when you're being supported... It's awful both ways."— *"My days of pleasing men are over!"*
— *Little Edie Bouvier, Grey Gardens*

But let me take you back to the beginning, before any of that. Long before I opened my own brothel, long before I knew how to navigate the sex industry in a professional manner, I'd acquired a job at a massage parlor I discovered while turning the pages in the Village Voice. Madams lit up hearing my British public school girl accent, assuming it meant class and education.

My aversion to fluorescent lights and the soul-crushing blandness of corporate life was as strong as my need for a steady cash flow. I simply wasn't built for that particular brand of slow, agonizing office job type death. I craved something else entirely. I needed to be a part of a world brimming with characters, with stories, with a real view of humanity. So, with no experience except my background in styling hair and makeup, I searched for an off-the-grid type of job. That's when this ad caught my eye.

ADULT HELP WANTED! Female Models needed for gentleman's massage spa. No Exp. Nec. Will Train! CASH! Midtown loc. Call Ms. Josephine 352 7891

I wasted no time and called the phone number.

Over the next few days, I fantasized who Josephine was and what she looked like. I formed a picture of a slender, petite, pale yet rosy-skinned glamorous woman dressed in a Victorian dressing gown, with wavy red hair to her waist. She would take long drags from a European cigar, smoking it out of a long ivory and silver holder. Her breath would hold a faint aroma of violets. This was my preconceived romantic notion of what a traditional madam and brothel owner looked like. I had no other references.

As a child, I had watched the 1972 film Cabaret, starring Joel Grey and Liza Minnelli, over and over, probably close to a hundred times. There was something about that film that moved me at a very young age. I felt a connection, a fascination, drawn to that style of life. I'm certain I had wandered the streets of Weimar Berlin in a previous existence.

Anyway, my mother had actually blamed that film for me being who I was and would become.

The address Josephine had given me on the phone was directly across from Carnegie Hall and the legendary Russian Tea Room, on 57th Street and Broadway.

I inhaled city-fresh air and pulled open the old heavy glass doors. I waited in the lobby for the elevator to take me to the eighth floor. There, I knocked on a door marked three.

I was greeted by a 6-foot-tall, mousy, curly, short-haired woman of around forty. She invited me into the "studio," as she referred to her brothel.

Josephine's real name was Marge, I later discovered. She had a soft-spoken Scottish brogue that might have been enhanced, but that was just good business. Her accent was part of her image.

Josephine was the most unlikely prostitute and madam I could imagine. All my preconceived ideas were squashed when I walked into my first New York City brothel.

Josephine's eyes focused deeply into mine, searching and taking me in. Straight away, I felt I was in the right place, and she made me feel comfortable.

Josephine showed me around the office she'd made

into a plain, discreet brothel. It was in a legitimate professional office building, on fashionable 57th Street, no less.

Once you entered through the front door, you stepped into a living room. There was the main room, with a desk where Josephine, or Evie the Saturday phone girl, sat answering phones and booking appointments. Two couches sat opposite each other, where we, the ladies, sat waiting for clients and reading magazines.

The studio was basic: three small bedrooms, and a tiny back room for us to store our belongings, eat lunch, and smoke cigarettes out of the city blackened, soot-covered window.

In each room, there was a single sturdy massage table, a nightstand, and a chair. The usual bottle of rubbing alcohol, lotion, KY, and tissues were placed inside a drawer. A long mirror hung on a wall in each room, and that was it. No fairy lights or red-light bulbs, and no cheap "sexy" art posters. If anyone accidentally walked into the office, no one would suspect anything unusual was going on. Well, except for the three or four "scantily clad" women standing around.

"So, dearie, I must ask, have you done work like this before? Because it's fine if you haven't, we will train you. You do know what we do here, don't you?" Josephine began.

"Well, I think so. I've had some experience working the street in Earls Court, London a few years ago, but that was different. I have also worked as a phone girl for an escort service here in New York." I was trying to sell my worldly experience.

Let me fill you in on that experience. As teenagers, my best friend Penny and I had discovered the world of prostitution, all on our own. We needed money for our baby heroin habits. On Earls Court High

Street, not far from my parents' Chelsea home, you couldn't walk a block without being propositioned by one of the many Arab men lazily strolling the area. They were easily distinguishable: long white cotton pajamas, leather flip-flops, and turbans. And we, being teenagers and fresh meat, thought we'd stumbled into a seemingly bottomless bucket of easy cash.

There was an undeniable allure to the entire exchange, something I found utterly irresistible. Perhaps a past life memory, etched deep into my soul, was stirring once again.

My best friend and I were learning the shrewd art of prostitution. We watched the other teenage junkies, following their suit, as they pulled punters for their drugs too. We soon unearthed a method for finding enough cash to satisfy our baby habits. On a few occasions we'd slip into large, fancy apartment buildings, wandering the quiet halls, pressing our ears to doors, listening for any sign of a male voice within. If a male voice echoed from behind a door, we knocked. It took us ten minutes to fulfill the transaction and get paid. And it felt, truly, fantastic. What other teenager could conjure cash with such ease? Every ill-gotten penny melted into our young arms. But I was hooked, not just on the gear itself, but on the very means of its acquisition.

But this job at Josephine's wasn't ripping off unsuspecting Arabs on Earls Court High Street. This was a real job. No robbing was necessary. We provided a service that was in demand, as the endless ringing telephone suggested.

"Oh, well that's nice. So, you understand we charge for adult services? $100 for the hour, and $60 for the half. They will tip you the same as the house fee, and anything you do after the massage is up to you and your client. And I know you're going to do very well here." She smiled and reached for the ringing phone. "Good afternoon, and how can I help you, sir? Ah, hello Bill. Yes, Lily is here. 3 p.m. sweetheart? Wonderful, see you then. Bub-bye" she purred. "Lily 3pm sweetie, it's Bill." She winked. "Ah goodie." Lily scrunched her eyes up smiling.

"I have a very loyal customer base, and we only place a select few advertisements. I like to keep my studio small. I ask all my ladies to dress conventionally when coming and going, so we don't invite any unwanted attention from our neighbors. How many days would you like to work, dearie?" I had to hide my growing addiction. So far,

Josephine seemed to have not noticed my pinned pupils lost in my deep brown eyes, but I had to be careful.

"I'd like to work four days," I said tentatively, not wanting to appear too desperate and give up how desperate I truly was.

"Really, just four?" Josephine queried.

"Well, can I work more?"

"You can work as much as you like, but why don't you take six days?" She was already penciling me in. "Sounds good to me." I was ecstatic. "Wonderful. We close Sundays, and Evie will be here on Saturdays to answer the phones. You'll love her, and it might just be the two of you. We close at 4 PM instead of 7 PM on Saturday." She lit a cigarette and reached for the ringing phone.

"Good morning, ahh Sam. Yes, actually, I do have a new lady who's going to be joining us. She's sitting right in front of me: long dark hair, with alabaster skin, 34C, 24, 36, and she's British! Oh, Sam, you are a flirt, but I think Tiffany will be an excellent selection. She's just your type, I know what you like, don't I? She's twenty-one," (I was eighteen) "and she's totally new to the business, yes, brand new."

Josephine winked at me. "She's with me now. Oh Bill, you naughty man." She teased and flirted. "I'm making up her schedule now, but why don't you come in tomorrow, to be her first!" In her best Glaswegian brogue, Josephine had a knack. Hell, I'd be sold too!

"Now one rule is no pants," she said, rubbing the knee of my leather jeans and smiling. "And please be punctual. Bring your own condoms, as I charge $2 per if you forget them, and $5 for KY. I suggest purchasing a packet of finger condoms from Duane Reade. They sell them there, don't they, Lily?" Josephine asked a quiet woman sitting opposite.

An attractive, slightly older Asian woman, Lily, who'd been sitting across from Josephine's desk reading Cosmopolitan. She maybe in her early thirties, she took off her large round glasses and said in an accent, "Yeah, I just bought some. You wanna get some of these, because the men, they like the finger in the butt-butt. You know."

She giggled like a girl, covering her mouth and scrunching her eyes. Lily held her index finger up and rolled what looked like a miniature condom onto it.

"Get finger condom, you don't want no dirty fingernails inside the client's butt. Very important for safety and hygiene!" Lily said matter-of-factly in her soft Korean accent.

"Goo goo in your nail, agh!!! Ha ha! No no goo goo! The men like you to put finger in butt hole." She continued giggling, clearly amusing herself. "Ah, well thanks for the tip, I'll pick some up." Truth was, I hadn't been asked, as of yet, to put my fingers in anyone's butt hole, but like I said, "yet."

The interview went splendidly, and I was offered a job! I felt unbelievably proud and confident, and looked forward to this new adventure and career. This wasn't low-end street hustling on Earls Court High Street with my best friend. No, this was a career.

And I planned on turning it into one. I could work as much as I wanted. I took six days to start; I needed that $200 a day. This wasn't the chaotic randomness of escort work, running around at all hours. This was structured. I could work days and shoot dope evenings. Win-win. Of course, drugs were forbidden at Josephine's. But I was already an expert at hiding my addiction. Being an addict is so shameful. I settled into my new professional world, tracks carefully concealed with layers of makeup, ready to perfect my craft.

A 90-YEAR-OLD PIMP

"Green for the money, gold for the honey."
— Bishop Magic Don Juan

In the absence of a flickering TV screen, the back room of Josephine's studio became our personal confessional booth, a dimly lit sanctuary with a washing machine always churning. We didn't need Netflix. We had each other, a diverse group of women swapping tales of past lives, childhood traumas, and the ever-elusive dream of a future where you didn't have to explain to your family what you "do."

Between clients, we'd huddle in that cramped space, surrounded by bottles of Ivory bubble bath, (Josephine used it instead of actual bubble bath, because it was cheaper) and the rhythmic thump of wet towels spinning endlessly. It was there, amidst whispered confessions and shared cigarettes, that the most fascinating characters of my new world revealed themselves.

Josephine, our resident romance novel connoisseur, was living proof that beauty standards are, shall we say, flexible in the world of paid companionship. At six feet tall, with the posture of a question mark and a complexion that suggested a permanent blush, she was hardly a pin-up. But as the old saying goes, there's a lid for every pot, and Josephine had her devoted clientele back in the day, and now she'd shuffled them over to us. Evie, our sweet-as-sugar Saturday phone girl, was another testament to the vast and wonderfully weird depths of this industry.

But it was in this cramped old New York office building that I stumbled upon one of the more delightful anomalies of my career: Mr. Duvall, the 90-year-old pimp. And trust me, when I say 90,

I'm not exaggerating. He was probably a bit older. The man was a walking antique, a relic from an era when pimping still required a certain elegance from another world.

He's French, real French, not that Canadian

French nonsense. He speaks with a heavy accent and charmingly mangled English that's so perfectly; stereotypically French. He only wears suits, old tailored numbers that now have a shine to the seat and hang a little loosely off his bony shoulders. When he shuffles into the office, he's sporting what appear to be rather large, custom-made brown leather shoes, shined and buffed to perfection, no doubt by one of the increasingly obsolete shoe-shine boys who works outside Grand Central. I watched him from the corner of my eye, moving from the closet where he'd hung his overcoat across the small room to Josephine's desk. That journey alone could take a full minute.

Mr. Duvall showed up every other day, slowly navigating the office on thin, pencil-like legs that looked so fragile. Rita, our beautiful Donna Summer look alike and office gossip, informed me he'd been in the garment industry and had done well for himself. This brothel business was just a fun side game, you know, casual pimping. He wore a hat, tilted ever so slightly, and when it rained, he'd produce a sleek, tightly wrapped umbrella with a wooden duck's head handle. He also carried a shiny gold pocket watch that he kept in his breast pocket. I appreciated his quality accessories and admired his old-world style.

He adored Josephine and undoubtedly relished looking at the young women and soaking up the flirtatious attention we gave him. Who could blame him? I really hoped I wasn't going to be asked to give him a session, though. I'd seen plenty of elderly gentlemen since working in the sex industry, but never quite this ancient. I'm certainly no ageist. In fact, the older clients are often preferable. They don't want to fuck like rabbits for an hour. The mature gentleman typically is gentle and just wants to see and touch young skin, and he's so grateful to have a woman be sensual and kind. However, seeing Mr. Duvall in his undies would be just wrong. Some boundaries exist for everyone's psychological well-being.

One of my private clients was Jean Luc, who was equally ancient. He could have been a hundred. He'd owned a well-established, old-school French restaurant for forty-odd years, where equally elderly Upper East Side New Yorkers could dine with their families. It had become one of those soon-to-be-obsolete New York institutions. The food was good, not excellent, but decent. Jean, as I called him, liked to take me there, and we'd sit in a low-lit booth for lunch. His staff would stare at me, and I was fine with it because it genuinely gave Jean pleasure to be seen with a young woman. There's something endearing about an old man's simple pride in female companionship. He told me his restaurant was going to close soon. Business was down, he said, because all his customers were dying off. I understood the mathematics of mortality in his world.

Afterward, we'd catch a cab just a few blocks to his large, old apartment off Central Park East. Jean didn't want sex in any conventional sense. He wanted me to lie next to him, touch him, hold him. I could feel his loose skin reacting to my fingers. He'd shiver with a rash of goosebumps, yearning for touch more than orgasm.

One time I fell asleep. I was mortified, but he was overjoyed! Jean thought it a total compliment that I was so comfortable I could fall asleep in his bed. Truth was, I'd nodded the fuck out, I think. But who needs to know the truth? Exactly, he didn't. I'm only telling you.

Eventually, I stopped receiving calls from Jean Luc and assumed he'd passed. I genuinely enjoyed my time with him. He made me feel safe and cared for in a parental way. I bet he was a good dad.

Back at the studio, Rita filled me in on Mr. Duvall's history. He'd been a good client of Josephine's back in the day. When she'd suggested opening her own place, Mr. Duvall had given her the cash and, more importantly, a legitimate cover story, and he could forge a legal LLC for Josephine's taxes. It gave him purpose, and he loved visiting the studio to look over the books, what better job for an elderly gentleman, and he was a gentleman in every sense of the word. It was an unusual setup, but productive. The old man got his kicks playing puppet master to a small empire of female entrepreneurs, and Josephine got financial backing without having to explain her business model to traditional investors. I watched and learned as much as I could from everyone in that strange ecosystem. Here was proof that the sex industry, like any other business, required investors, accountants, and business plans. It just happened that our board meetings took place between a washing machine and a stack of towels, and our CEO wore custom leather shoes and checked a gold pocket watch. There was something beautifully absurd about Mr. Duvall, this ancient Frenchman who'd found purpose in his golden years by bankrolling a brothel. In a world where retirement usually meant golf and early bird specials, he'd chosen to become an entrepreneur in the oldest profession. It was either the most inspiring or most disturbing career pivot one could imagine.

Probably both.

THE HOOKER
THERAPY SESSIONS

*"Children are not born addicts, they become addicts
through their environment and experiences."*
—*Gabor Mate*

This was 1986 in New York City, just before Giuliani cleaned up the streets. Mayor Koch still reigned supreme, and I was never more starstruck than when I ran into him at a Greek restaurant in Queens. Gracious and surprisingly tall, he had my instant admiration.

At Josephine's, I was introduced to Tim Duff, a client who would teach me more about human nature than any textbook ever could. We always called them "clients," sometimes "tricks" or "dates." In London, we said "punters." I never use "johns." It feels like media shorthand from a different era.

Tim was short, maybe five-three in Cuban heels, and morbidly obese. He looked like he'd swallowed a tire, carrying tremendous weight disproportioned to his small frame. Yet somehow, he pulled off an aura of sophistication with thousand-dollar suits, buffed nails, and expensive cologne. His shirts were crisply pressed, his few hair strands carefully combed and held with hairspray. His initials were embroidered on his cuffs. He was a character the women all knew and liked, a frequent flyer for years.

Josephine made it clear on my first day: clients never see each other. Not in hallways, not in the lounge, not even in doorknob reflections. In this regard, the place resembled a therapist's office, and my work would prove therapy-adjacent in ways I hadn't expected. A couch, a listening ear, transactional intimacy. The main difference was insurance didn't cover our sessions and there was no pressure or pretense of getting better.

Some working women say men pay them to talk, and I've had clients who didn't want penetration. But generally, this work requires sexual service of some kind. Whether dominance sessions with tools and costumes, stress-relieving massages with hand releases (popular with the lunchtime crowd), or two-girl lesbian shows, any scenario could be arranged.

And then of course we have the water sports crowd. You'd be surprised at the men I've encountered who want to be peed and shit upon. The latter I was able to fake with a warmed-up Hershey bar that happened to have nuts in it.

This particular gentleman was an outrageous alcoholic and he wanted me to wear his white cotton underwear and poop in them. While he was half unconscious, I was able to slip the bar of chocolate out from my own underwear and as it had been pressed between my cheeks for the past hour, it was all melted and gross. I opened the foil wrapped bar and smeared it in the cotton briefs and tried to wave away the Hershey giveaway chocolate whiff. He bought it. Not once but five times. At six hundred dollars a poop I thought I was extremely savvy. Then I think Ashley told him my secret and that was that.

But back to Josephine's, I was eager to learn from these older women, the kind I'd searched for since childhood, hoping they existed. What I really wanted was a mother figure who'd teach me to navigate this difficult world. My mother's own "motherhood" seemed to end at my conception. But I had these women now, and Josephine was the next best thing to a mum. She was kind to me and I felt safe, maybe even cared for. Rita introduced me to Tim. "Say hello to Tiffany," she said. Ridiculous name, I know. It sounded like a Connecticut senator's trust-fund baby.

Josephine named me after her newborn daughter. I surmised if she loved the name, she would book me more often. It worked. Slipping into that identity let me play someone else: undamaged, not an addict fleeing my abusive and neglectful British family. I wanted a fresh start, and to discover who I was. I wanted to be pure.

The moment we shook hands, Tim's head lowered and he switched into a shy, childlike demeanor, talking in what he assumed was a little boy's voice but sounded more like someone with severe speech disabilities. We watched him slip his tie over his head, keeping the knot intact. He slowly unbuttoned his starched shirt, revealing a clean white undershirt, then stepped out of massively wide pants, laying them neatly over the chair. Standing in calf-length socks with garters and an undershirt tucked into baggy boxers, Mr. Duff was quite the sight. I'd never seen sock garters before. They looked arcane and uncomfortable, though no more than women's garters, only those are considered sexy.

The scenario never varied: Rita and I played "Timmy's" mean governesses, sexually molesting poor young Timmy. We'd tease in mocking tones, poke and play with his genitals, laugh at him. Eventually we'd masturbate him to orgasm, just as his governess had all those years ago. I'd noticed a pattern with successful, wealthy businessmen who wanted severe domination, often with scripts planned to minute details. When I asked why this turned them on, I learned that men who gave orders all day, in charge of vast sums or stress-inducing titles, found satisfaction being on the receiving end for an hour. A release from responsibility. They could strip down to boxers and gartered socks, be molested and ridiculed to orgasm, knowing their secrets were safe with us.

Afterward, Duff would put his still-knotted tie

back over his head like a boy, then promptly switch back to the boss, the big man. Only we working women know what powerful men running the world are really made of.

At first, I was shocked, later saddened by what we were instructed to do. I realized Duff's scenario had repeated for decades with no plan to stop his "therapy" sessions. We'd poke his thick, pimpled back, taunt and mock his body, push him between us while he feigned distress. You could see his thorough enjoyment, which made me up the ante. I discovered I enjoyed being cruel to him, and he loved that. Finding myself enjoying this torment was disturbing. I'm an empath to the highest order, yet here was a side I never knew existed. Stripped to baggy boxers, unbuttoned shirt, and undershirt, Duff appeared oddly childlike with his head hung low, arms folded over his massive belly. His practiced demeanor was what disturbed me most. After forty-five minutes of mild abuse, Rita instructed Timmy onto the bed. We continued molesting him, playing with his penis and nipples, pinching and pulling pubes, mocking his masculinity. I pressed my finger to my lips. "Shush, don't tell anyone, Timmy. It's our secret." I saw his eyes glaze with familiar bliss. Rita finished him while I fake-laughed at his fake discomfort. Total theater. Duff paid well. We each made $250 for that hour without undressing, and Tim never touched us.

Over time, Tim opened up about the nanny who'd molested him as a child, how that became his ultimate sexual fantasy. He'd discovered his therapy was reenacting trauma. Traditional therapy did nothing. He enjoyed coming to us because we soothed that internal itch only he knew how to scratch. The scenario was deliberate and safe. He knew exactly what to expect. I repeat situations and behaviors because that's what trauma does. It lives inside our bodies, becomes part of our entire being. Tim dealt with his molestation as best he could understand. It wasn't that deep. I'd hear similar stories for decades. Just varied trauma in the duffel bag of damage we all carry. If you can find the root and live with it comfortably, that's the best we can do. He pressed a neatly folded hundred into my palm. "See you next week," with a wink.

Watching Tim week after week, I began understanding something crucial about this work, about trauma, about the strange ways we all seek healing. In my isolation, shooting dope alone in my apartment. Tim, in his elaborate rituals, was trying to transform his. Neither of us was getting traditional therapy, but we were both finding ways to survive.

Maybe that's all any of us can do. Find our own twisted path to feeling human again, even if it leads through the strangest territories imaginable.

THE LADIES AND A REAL LIVE NYMPHOMANIAC

"I've been absolutely terrified every moment of my life — and I've never let it keep me from doing a single thing I wanted to do. — Georgia O'Keeffe

Here's the thing about irony: at eighteen, I was working in a brothel with a strict "no drugs" policy. Which was actually expected, and considering my professional-level relationship with controlled substances. Our esteemed madam, Josephine, I discovered was in recovery herself. So, every lunchtime, I perfected my performance by spinning tales of virtuous NA meetings on St. Marks Place, claiming I was dutifully filing into the old Electric Circus like some newly reformed pilgrim. In reality, my daily pilgrimage took me somewhere far less spiritual on the Lower East Side. I'd step off the subway at Eighth and Broadway and stroll along St. Marks, nodding to the usual characters, locals hawking dog-eared paperbacks and odds-and-ends on fold-out tables, the scent of incense drifting from a head shop, a battered boombox blasting Purple Rain into the cold downtown city air. Scruffy junkie-punks hunched near Second Avenue, rattling cups for spare change, and I noticed a young couple I'd seen around for years now pushing a stroller—life insisting on happening even in that bleak, Reagan-era backdrop. Navigating that tightrope while maintaining my meticulous illusion of functional sobriety required a certain flair.

But let's talk about the real show: the other women.

I was the youngest at eighteen. Most were at least ten years older, and every single one was a character. Lily was a thirty-or-forty-something Asian woman who would never, ever give up that information. She was sexy, really funny, and didn't know how cool she was. Newly married to a younger man she said was "straight off the boat," but she still went to Atlantic City alone every week to gamble for hours. Lottery tickets, poker, all of it. She lived to gamble. I really enjoyed everything about her.

Nicky was a thirty-something lesbian with short blond hair and that minimal makeup effort you know, clear mascara and lip gloss. I appreciated it. She looked thoroughly awkward in a skirt, since Josephine insisted "no pants" while working. Nicky had a beautiful, exotic-looking wife who went to school while Nicky worked to support her. We became friends, even went out to eat a couple of times. Abigail was a round, Midwestern twenty-something and the youngest besides me. She rarely looked people in the eye, just twirled her hair and stared at the ground when you tried to talk to her. Shy as hell. She preferred to stay in an empty room reading novels all day. She was also going to school for psychology. Make of that what you will.

Then there was Lena. You see, Lena was special. Very special. And she was treated as such. Because Lena was a real-live nymphomaniac. Lena came in when she wanted and was booked back-to-back with only regulars. She was thin and blond, her hair trimmed in a conservative straight bob that curled under her jaw. Thirty-five, college educated, and a runner. She ran in New York City marathons. She also had a Wall Street corporate job. And she came to Josephine's three times a week out of physical necessity. She simply had to have sex. Lots of it. The clients who were fortunate enough to meet Queen Lena when she was taking new clients, they hadn't looked at another whore since. She gave them the full GFE (girlfriend experience). Her sessions were real. Must have been exhausting. When Lena came out of her session room to use the bathroom, she was red-faced, hair all knotted in the back after an hour of fucking the crap out of some regular Romeo. She made the big bucks, and we all just stared at her.

Here's the kicker: Lena thought she was better than us. She thought we were the lowly working women. We were whores. She wasn't, apparently. She couldn't relate to us, and I couldn't relate to her, not for her nymphomania, but because she was just a snobby white woman. And not a soul in her corporate world would imagine that she was fucking and sucking countless strangers, one after the other, during her work week, and loving it. Oh, and yes, Lena was married. Her husband knew she worked in a brothel and apparently understood her needs. I'm sure he didn't mind the extra two hundred-plus grand she brought in yearly, tax-free. And he no doubt couldn't deliver her insatiable sexual desires on his own. She was unique in this world of uniqueness.

Everyone else was kind and welcoming. I'm not just saying that. Josephine had somehow managed to assemble a perfect crew. Not one bad apple. Yet. Surrounded by Lily's gambling tales, Nicky's friendship, Abigail's quiet sweetness, and Lena's utterly unhinged yet undeniably profitable sex drive, I began to understand something: Josephine's little studio was more than just a brothel. It was a wonderfully dysfunctional, surprisingly kind family. A collection of women, each with our own secrets and vices and a shared understanding that the shame society heaps upon us was never really ours to carry. Even Lena's snobbery felt more amusing than offensive. Because in the end, we were all just women finding our own cracks to let the light in.

THE TALE OF A TAIL

"I slept with faith and found a corpse in my arms on awakening; I drank and danced all night with doubt and found her a virgin in the morning."
— Aleister Crowley

It reminded me why I'd chosen this path in the first place, why I'd traded conventional safety for the raw uncertainty of life on society's margins. Sometimes you need to look backward to understand how far you've traveled forward. Let me take you back a few years, to when I was still learning the ropes, still figuring out just how deep the rabbit hole could go. I was working for an escort service called "Through the Keyhole," run by a woman named Dot. Back then, I thought I'd seen everything, done everything for a buck. I had no idea how naive I was.

The phone rang at 3 am on a cold Manhattan winter night. I was living on 9th Avenue and 14th Street, in a drafty old loft right above the Hellfire Club, and I knew exactly who was calling. Anne, my roommate and the phone girl for the service, was the only person who'd be reaching out at this ungodly hour.

"Zoe, hi, hey girl, you awake? Get up... I got a live one!"

"What time is it?" I mumbled, though

I was already fully dressed, waiting for her call. The only call I'd be getting at 3 am. "It's 3:15 and you have twenty minutes to be at The Milford Plaza hotel on 8th Avenue. Room 711. His name is Jeffrey Short, and Dot says he's a special client. No sex... don't say it, I know what you're thinking."

"Total freak, right?"

"That's what you always tell me.

Now move your ass, love you."

I hated the 3 am calls.

The cold slapped my face as I stepped onto the blackened, slushy pavement. The streets were dead, lit only by one street lamp illuminating a few snowflakes drifting through the morning chill. 14th Street had turned into a skating rink, and I was already regretting my leather pumps as I frantically waved down a cab. Miraculously, I arrived on time and knocked on room 711. A tall, thin, pale man opened the door immediately, like he'd been waiting at the peephole.

"Mr. Short? I'm Zoe."

I stepped inside, scanning everything the way I always did. Wallet, shoes, watch, coins, briefcase, and a bag by the bed. Everything seemed normal, but in this business, nothing is normal. And yet everything abnormal becomes normal after a while. You understand, don't you? Of course you do.

"Moneys on the dresser. Take it. Do you have to call Dotty?"

We called our boss "Dot," not "Dotty," and I found it charming that he'd added the cute "y" to her straightforward name. I'd been with so many different men, and they usually acted nervous, eager to begin. It's an awkward few moments you learn to navigate. Imagine meeting a total stranger, then stripping naked to tend to their sexual needs as casually as being asked to pass the salt.

"What's your name again?"

"Zoe," I repeated, my smile purposely not reaching my eyes. I was still checking him out, on high alert.

"Dotty said you'd be okay with what I like to do. It's not sex, so don't worry." He kept looking at my feet, stealing swift glances at me. "I'm Jeffrey."

"Lovely to meet you. In town on business?" The conversation I'd had repeatedly. Where are you from? What brings you to New York? Then we'd dance around the weather.

Prostitution had taught me life skills I might never have learned otherwise. One is how to fuck like a professional.

Everyone knows how to fuck. We're animals, after all. But I'm talking about turning this favorite pastime into a career, learning to be so good that men keep coming back, paying you extremely well for your time and expertise. They buy you cars, houses, everything in between. All because you now know how to fuck like a whore. But back to Jeffrey, he was different. Well over six feet tall, weighing maybe 130 pounds, shoulders hunched forward, and his left eye had a drifty thing, and kept sliding outwards. As I fetched the money off the dresser, I was startled by what sounded like a rodent clawing in the top drawer. "Jeffrey, what's... I think there's something in this drawer..." His icy, skeletal fingers touched my hand, making me shudder. "Don't look. You can trust me, can't you?" He had a slight lisp. "Dotty knows. You won't be in any danger." Yeah, I'd heard that line before. He pulled out a hand mirror with thick lines already cut. "It's crystal," he said, biting his lower lip and twitching his nose. I generally didn't like crystal meth. It was cheaper, harsher than coke. I'd done it plenty in London during the '80s, I'd thrown a bump into my dope spoon to keep from nodding out at family dinners. Jeffrey inhaled two fat lines, then offered me the straw. I declined, it's hard for me to turn down any type of drugs, but one thing I knew for sure was that crystal would rip the last smidgen of heroin from my blood and make me a paranoid wreck. Out of the drawer, Jeffrey picked up a small wooden box covered with a handkerchief. By the end of this hour, I would have truly seen it all. I watched him peek under the cloth while making obscenely strange kissing noises. What in the holy rat lover's hell had I gotten myself into? Sensing my hesitation, Jeffrey said, "Listen, I'll give you an extra two hundred. It's easy. Let me explain what I'd like you to do." His excitement and attention to detail was remarkable. "I want you to open the box by my anus." "Your... anus?" I repeated, wide-eyed, making sure I understood correctly. "You lift the sliding door, pressed right against my anus. I want to feel the box on my buttocks so I know it's going to get into me... and let the mouse crawl up my asshole. Is that a problem? Dotty said it wouldn't be a problem." He looked blankly at me as one eye drifted left. I don't want to appear prudish, but this was highly unusual. And okay, I'll say it: it's a little gross. This had to be a test, right? Let's see how the fancy London girl handles the "rodent up the bum game." Dot and Anne must be having a laugh. Surely this was a joke. I smiled, waiting for him to say, "Got you!" But he didn't. I searched his stern face, scanned his stubbly chin and the two moles under his wonky eye. Not a hint of humor. He was deadly serious.

"It's easy. You will do it, won't you? How about I throw in an extra hundred on top of the two hundred, making it a three-hundred-dollar tip?"

Did I even have to think about it? I could be bought for the right amount, and not even that much. I wasn't sure if I felt sorrier for the rodent or myself. I knelt at the foot of the bed as Jeffrey crouched on all fours, his naked, wrinkled, stinking asshole sticking up in the air like some kind of incubus from hell.

I held the wooden box containing a small rodent. There was indeed a sliding door at one end. I was instructed to lift it slowly, with the box touching Jeffrey's asshole. If all went as planned, the rodent would scratch and burrow into his butt, giving him some sort of delight only he and other anal canal fetishists would understand. Rodents can claw the inside of the anal cavity and create spectacular damage, a fact I could have lived without knowing. Jeffrey positioned himself naked on the multicolored bedspread. I lifted the sliding wooden door and glimpsed a thin white mouse, its whiskers twitching as it sniffed at Jeffrey's asshole.

I turned my head away. The stench made my eyes water. I love animals, and this was horrific. Could I cancel now? I didn't think I could go through with this. I tried to think about other things. Christmas, hot chocolate, cooking up a hit. Heroin was my love, my only safety, my constant that took life's pain and reality away. I didn't want to think about what I was doing or what this tiny creature was going through. At that moment, I hated humans. We're sick animals, the cruelest species, willing to inflict suffering on anyone or anything for orgasmic satisfaction. I lifted the sliding door, holding the box at Jeffrey's asshole, and turned my head. The sensation of the heavy rodent scrambling to enter Jeffrey's body was too much. I almost quit right then, almost grabbed his money and split. But I didn't. I stayed, with my head turned as far away as possible. Jeffrey started breathing heavily. I saw him reach for his dangling balls and yank at his penis. The mouse had entered his body. After a few minutes, the mouse was no longer in the container. I placed the box on the bed. Now what? I tried to unhear the nauseating moans as he masturbated, his eyes firmly shut, groaning into mouthfuls of stained hotel pillow. I hoped he wasn't having a heart attack. I had to look. I turned quickly, hair over one eye, and peeked out. What I saw, I'll never forget or unsee. Jeffrey was face down in the pillow, his bony ass up in the air, and the tail of the mouse was hanging out of his asshole. I heaved, sweated, felt ill. My eyes watered, vomit rose in my throat, and then, without warning... I burst out laughing. It came out as a weird, high-pitched explosion from nowhere, a totally involuntary, hilarious cackle. Jeffrey lifted his head to look at me. Seeing his pale face flushed pink, mouth full of hotel pillow, bony butt still up in the air, and a mouse tail dangling from his gnawed and bleeding asshole, it was just too much. I had one of those dreadfully uncontrollable belly laughs. I tried to think of sad things to stop myself, but nothing worked. I went to the bathroom and splashed water on my face. But as soon as I looked in the mirror, the image of that tail dangling from his butt made me crack up all over again. I couldn't stop. Tears ran down my face, mixing with my black mascara. And if you're still with me, dear reader, he wasn't finished yet. He continued biting the pillow and masturbating his small, soft knob with his left hand. Two minutes after the rodent had burrowed into his body, Jeffrey came in the most unspectacular drip I'd ever seen, a little dollop as he heaved one last gurgle and slumped face-first on the bed.

The mouse was clearly dead. I hadn't thrown up, so it was time to go. Jeffrey carefully maneuvered off the bed without saying anything. I sat on the chair by the window, which I'd tried to open. But hotels nail them shut. Too many people tossing themselves out, I'd heard. Jeffrey began to prance around the hotel room, swaying his hips, posing, flicking the tiny tail from his asshole and twirling it around his fingers. "Do you like my quaint little tail, Miss Zoe?" Oh, hell no.

I went along with the game. What did I care? The worst seemed over, the mouse evidently dead, Jeffrey parading his mouse tail, and I hadn't thrown up. I considered it a well-earned hour of work. I made $650 and left swiftly before being asked to remove the dead rodent. Walking back through those same dark streets to cop my dope, I felt something shift inside me. The cold didn't bite as sharply, and my ruined leather pumps didn't seem to matter anymore. Six hundred and fifty dollars richer, I'd crossed a line I didn't even know existed.

That night with Jeffrey Short taught me something crucial about this business, about myself, about the lengths people will go to for pleasure, for money, for survival. I'd laughed in the face of something that should have disgusted me, and that laughter had saved me. It was my body's way of protecting my sanity, of finding light in the absolute darkness of human depravity.

Years later, when I was running Sterling Ladies, when I was making the rules instead of following them, I'd remember that mouse tail dangling in a hotel room at 4 am. I'd remember how laughter could be a form of resistance, how finding the absurd in the obscene could keep you human when everything else tried to strip that away. That's the thing about this life. It teaches you that survival isn't just about enduring. Sometimes it's about finding the humor in hell, about laughing until your mascara runs and your stomach aches, about walking away with your dignity intact even when the world tries to take that too.

SUCK DON'T BLOW

"Heroin was a love story, a seduction, a long, drawn-out goodbye." — Jerry Stahl, Permanent Midnight

I'm connected to my ancestors and the Goddess, to whom I've been devoted since my early teens. It's a connection that runs deeper than words can express, woven into the very fabric of who I am. Drawn to the Wiccan religion by something I couldn't quite name at the time, I became fascinated by the idea of manifesting desires and staying in touch with Mother Nature. I often felt the urge to wash myself in a river or bury myself in the earth. I wanted, no, I needed to be pure, to cleanse my soul. To wash away past lives whose pain I was still slinging to. I needed grounding and had no idea how to achieve it.

That longing sent me on a quest to read everything I could find. I discovered books on ancient practices, lunar cycles, and the sacred feminine. I read Drawing Down the Moon by Margot Adler, The Witches' Bible by Janet and Stewart Farrar, works by Raymond Buckland, and, of course, Crowley, along with countless others in my ever-growing collection.

Those books gave me a sense of hope I could have a maternal figure, something I desperately needed during those formative years, someone to teach me. Even if she wasn't physically in front of me to hold my hand or wipe away my tears, I longed for someone to guide me through the chaos of adolescence and beyond. I wish I'd found her earlier.

It made perfect sense to me that Mother Nature would be the foundation of our world, the primal force from which all life springs. Greek and Norse deities became my focus, drawing me into their ancient mysteries. Spell making, candle carving, and anointing began as practices that felt deeply familiar, as if I had performed these rituals in past lives and was simply remembering rather than learning. I began crafting my own soaps, infusing them with herbs and essential oils, each batch a connection to something ancient, and I was driven to immerse myself in more of this.

I even followed old recipes, hearty, stew- like dinners inspired by ancient Wiccan traditions, filling my home with warm, earthy, aromatic scents that made me feel closer to the divine. I was also dabbling in a lot of acid during those early days of my introduction to the craft, maybe following Crowley, or maybe just following my own intuition telling me to experience it all as I learned. Honestly, I've never really enjoyed acid. I'd had a bad trip when I was thirteen that left a permanent shadow over the stuff.

I'm telling you about my interest in the craft because there's simply no other explanation for the way I've slipped out of the gnarliest disasters without so much as a ticket or a polite visit from the authorities. Well... except for the one time I called the cops on myself, but that's a story for later. My point is: there's no logical explanation for the ease with which I've dodged catastrophes. The only answer is this, I have a get-out-of-jail-free card inked onto my soul. A divine protection that's been with me through every storm.

We'd stopped for drinks at Alcatraz on Avenue A, where I bought a round of vodka shots from a slightly chubby, goth bartender with East Village attitude and straight black hair. She had a bad tattoo on her upper arm and told us she was in a band. "Ace of Spades" blasted from the jukebox as two regulars hunched over the sticky bar, one of them wearing a faded Ramones T-shirt that had absolutely seen better days. Every square has that same Ramones T-shirt. I've had one for years myself, never worn it, never lost it, just keep it around for luck now. I'd already copped a week's worth of heroin, an eight-ball of blow, and a few dimes of weed. Just supplies. Easily picked up on the L.E.S.

It was another hot, humid summer in the city, and the unmistakable aromas hung heavy in the stagnant air. The streets reeked of car exhaust, sweat, piss, and pizza. "We Are the World" or Madonna seemed to drift out of every bodega that summer. I noticed someone had spray-painted "Basquiat Lives" on a boarded-up storefront near Tompkins Square. Jean-Michel and I had met at a runway fashion show, when I was assisting for Christian, a well-known hairstylist, and I had cut his hair on a few occasions, pre-dreads. I wish I'd kept the napkin on which he'd drawn a face for me. I had cut Warhol's wig too, Stephen Sprouse who was a good friend had introduced us. Andy sat on a toilet seat in a cramped bathroom in a fancy hotel and I had tried my best to style his synesthetic wig hair. He was quiet and soft spoken and asked me about London and Catholic school. I had befriended the great Jimmy Page on a job for his band The Firm, but that's another story for later.

After drinks, we hit the road back upstate. It was late rush hour. West Side traffic inched uptown towards the George Washington Bridge.

The lights were harsh on my dope-pinned eyes. I focused intently on not weaving, trying to stay in my lane. I wasn't on the nod, but definitely nod-adjacent. Plus, I was buzzed from vodka shots and a pinch or three of L.E.S. blow, just to even me out for the drive.

No problem, until I saw the big sign ahead: "FIELD SOBRIETY TEST STOP" flashing in giant letters. I froze. A sharp, slow panic began to throb in my temples. Then I slammed into full-blown terror, sweat pouring down the back of my neck.

"Oh no! Hey guys, wake up, we are fucked!" I shook the sleeping passengers into hyper panic.

"Guys, they are gonna bust me! There's not a chance in hell I can pass a sobriety test. Larry, baby, you have to switch seats with me. Please, honey." I pleaded as I wiped my sweaty palms on my pants.

When cops pull us over, which seems to be rather often, Larry and I have a method to keep one of us, usually me, out of jail. While I'm driving, Larry slides into the driver's seat, positioning himself under me as I lift up slightly. I hold the wheel and keep my foot on the gas as he takes over the pedals. Then I slide over him into the passenger seat. If that sounds complicated and dangerous, it is, and I don't recommend it. But who considers danger when your freedom is at stake?

Somehow, I've always managed to avoid getting pinched. And, being a chivalrous guy, Larry always takes the fall for me. He went to jail on drug charges twice. If that isn't love, I don't know what is. Plus, Larry used his one phone call from jail to tell me where he'd hidden the dope in the car so I wouldn't be sick. Bless him.

Back home, I was a regular visitor at the Orange County jail, except for that one time they wouldn't let me in. They said I was too high.

But I'm getting ahead of myself.

"I can't change seats," Larry said. "I forgot to bring my license!"

"Damn it, Larry, what am I gonna do? I can't pass a fucking sobriety test. Why didn't you bring your license? Why am I the one always figuring stuff out? Can't you do anything? I have to do everything?" I wailed, wanting to blame him for whatever transpired.

"Don't freak out," he said, his voice surprisingly confident. "Just one step at a time. You always get away with these things."

Confidence I wasn't feeling at that precise moment.

"Don't be so sure, you might have jinxed me! Damn it, why did you say that? You just fuckin' jinxed me."

"Say what?" Larry asked.

"Oh nothing. Fuck, I'm going to jail."

"No, you're not. You're gonna be fine. Take a deep breath and pretend you are like a soccer mom, or something, you know, act normal." Brian leaned forward from the back seat and squeezed my arm.

"Soccer mom, what? This isn't funny, I'm going to jail, God damn it."

I was freaking out.

"I need to pee," Mike said to Brian.

"It's all that beer you drink, can you wait till we get through this?" Brian snapped.

The red and orange lights made me squint as we inched towards the sobriety site. My head was pounding. Deep breaths, anxiety streaming through my blood. I gobbled a fistful of Altoids, preparing myself for whatever lies I'd have to think up on the spot.

One officer waved at me to pull over to the side, while the car in front of us was let go. Fuck. I'm done. This is it.

Another cop walked over to the car. I turned the CD player off. Playing *Fear No More*. This one was older, self-assured, with a short-cropped grey fade. He opened my car door. I smiled, but it probably looked more like a grimace. Plus, I was attempting to chew the Altoids and probably foaming at the mouth.

I got out, struggling to act as steady and as conventional as possible. Vodka swirled in my gut and brain, along with enough narcotics to put a rhino down for the count. I looked up at the polluted night skies and exhaled a long sigh.

It was about now that I became super self-conscious about my tight black Lip Service pants that spelled

"FUCK" all over them in a recurring pattern.

I kept Brian's soccer mom image in my head. If you feel it, you can be it. Soccer mom, soccer mom, normal, be normal, act NORMAL, look NORMAL, think NORMAL, whatever that is.

Everything slowed way down as I looked out over the ribbons of car lights streaming north and south.

I gazed over the roof of the car, vision blurry, and knew I was going directly to jail. I wasn't passing go, and I wasn't collecting two hundred dollars.

I followed the officer to the side of the highway, while rubbernecking travelers stared at me from their cars. Every single one of them, I figured, was thanking whatever god they believed in that they hadn't been pulled over.

The officer instructed me on how to blow into the small tube attached to the breathalyzer. I barely heard him; the traffic, the lights, and the blood in my head pounded so loudly. God, are you there? I need you now! Help me, Goddess. Anyone. Then, like a blast of divine inspiration, something inside me told me to SUCK, DO NOT BLOW! And suck I did. One, two, three. I waited. Just waited for the officer to give me the look, and angrily order me to re-do.

But instead... Something beautiful happened.

The officer, who might, I decided, be an angel in disguise, studied his breathalyzer machine. Into it, I had sucked, not blown. Seeing there was no number generated, he said, "Good-bye Miss, sorry for the hold-up, have a good night." I opened my mouth, but decided to say nothing. So, I simply turned, without looking up at him, without thanking him, without even breathing. Surely, he'd sniff the vodka and haul me off to Rikers.

All the heads in my car turned around, watching from the back window. And then I walked, or maybe floated, back to the car.

"Oh my God, I can't believe it. I can't believe what just happened," I said, shaking my head in disbelief.

I turned the car engine on and split.

"I literally have no fucking idea how or what just happened," I said. "I was already tasting the bologna sandwiches at Rikers."

"But, baby, what did you do?" Larry asked.

"Something told me to breathe in instead of blowing into the breathalyzer, and God damn it worked! It fucking worked!"

"Suck, don't blow. If that isn't a life lesson, what is?" Brian said.

To this day, I have no explanation for what happened that night. Or what happened in court after my Mercedes swan dived into the pool. Or on a thousand and one occasions when by all rights my number should have been up. Somehow, I'm still here. And your guess is as good as mine.

SUGAR DADDY

"I am not what happened to me, I am what I choose to become." — Carl Jung

What I craved most was a soft place to land. After years of hustling, surviving, and constantly looking over my shoulder, I wanted safety, though I didn't even know what that felt like anymore. My world had become a series of calculated risks, quick escapes, and the relentless pursuit of the next hit. Every day was about making it through that day, moment to moment, I didn't have the scope to ever see ahead. That's trauma.

The exhaustion wasn't just physical, though my body carried the weight of countless late nights and a decade of chemical abuse. You can live like that when you're young, it takes many decades to truly catch up with you, and as we know the human body can withstand incredible abuse. The true weariness was deeper: a soul-deep fatigue that came from the twice-daily pilgrimage to the Lower East Side, a ritual I'd maintained for a decade. It was my descent into the underworld for the medicine that bought me another few hours. My addiction dictated every breath, who I talked to, who I hung out with, and who I aspired to be. Survival mode had become so normal that I didn't realize its effect until I caught a breath of fresh air, took a good look around, and actually thought for a moment. That's when the weight of it all hit me: how long I'd been running, how far I'd fallen, how desperately I needed something resembling stability.

For me, that solace arrived in the most unlikely form: a client we in my world called a "sugar daddy." An OBGYN, no less. The irony wasn't lost on me: a man who brought life into the world, sustaining someone slowly killing herself.

I'd tried the straight route a couple of times. Back when I was still "functional," I took a brief detour as a photography studio receptionist through

the Village Voice classifieds. The funny thing was, I never had trouble getting hired. My British accent always charmed managers into offering me positions on the spot. But why clock forty hours a week in a soul-crushing office when I could make the same money in half a day providing "sexual satisfaction and relaxation"? The math was simple, even if the work wasn't.

The office was thoroughly uninspiring, made "colorful" only by the lecherous brothers who owned the place. The older brother was a garden gnome at 5'3", sporting thick, greasy, mousy curly hair. He'd orbit the young women in the office like a creepy satellite, his scent a malevolent fog of body odor, coupled with a perpetually sweating face and damp underarms. Poor bastard. This troll-man, however, I had the distinct pleasure of intimidating. My tenure there ended not with a resignation but with my quiet, unapologetic disappearance. That's how I rolled back then. I just vanished.

Meanwhile, my relationship with Valium had really blossomed. I'd never had a pill habit before. I went straight to heroin. But I learned that Valium amplified the dope and became a reliable crutch in those dark, early morning hours when a coke binge threatened to tip you into psychosis. Well, I lived in psychosis. The pills just made it less suicidal.

Those little blue V's proved incredibly handy, silently creeping into my routine and contributing to many an overdose. I'd often come to on the floor of Room 102 or in the hallway of my Chelsea Hotel apartment, a bruised elbow and hip my only clues. I'd have no memory of how I got there, only that an overdose had wiped the slate clean.

Here's where "The Doctor" enters the picture. He'd been bringing me full shopping bags of sample Valiums from his medical office. At the time, it was the best gift imaginable. Who else would fuel my boundless addiction so generously, delivering these little bliss tablets free with his weekly visits? Well, he did pay me generously, too. I never understood why an accomplished older

man who delivered babies all day wanted to spend so much time with a twenty-year-old junkie hooker, especially since he didn't use drugs, drink, or smoke weed. But there he was, dropping by the brothel and booking me out all day while I took naps and he sat in an uncomfortable chair reading The Wall Street Journal.

Of course, we had sex. It was basic. But then we talked, and I learned to care about him. I understood that even though I was thoroughly strung out and needed help, lots of it, this man also needed to be cared for.

Initially, he didn't appeal to me as a friend. He wasn't someone I was particularly drawn to or had anything in common with. He lived a straight life, and now he wanted adventure. He also wanted freedom from a bad marriage, which he soon got.

The Doctor showered me with anything I wanted. Clothing, though I didn't care for much unless it was a cutoff T-shirt and rubber or leather pants. Shoes? I only wore Frye boots. I drove his black Mercedes 300, and he bought me a cute white Jeep that I quickly destroyed. Then he bought me another one, and then another.

I picked out a lovely four-bedroom ranch-style house in Orange County on seven acres, with enough room for my best friend Brian and his boyfriend to stay indefinitely. I was given credit cards and as much cash as I wanted or needed. All of it went into my arm. All of it. I'd say close to a million dollars in four certifiably insane years.

The Doctor even set up a bank account just for my "daily supplements," which ran anywhere from $250 to $1,000 a day. Despite everything, I did care for him and grew to love him as a friend. How could I not care for a man who tried so hard to help me and yet had no idea what that actually meant? He tried in the only ways he knew how, and I just kept taking what I needed to breathe.

Back home, it was Brian, his boyfriend Mike, myself, and The Doctor. Oh, and a dozen or so cats, plus a Rottweiler named Jezebella. It was an unorthodox setup, but The Doctor loved it, and I loved my animals, and together we made our own strange, diverse household. The ranch-style home sat on seven acres of land, giving me the perfect surroundings to dive deeper into my chosen religion: Wicca.

In between bouts of extreme drug use, which at the time meant about two bundles of heroin, a gram or three of coke, and a bottle or two of vodka a day, I still managed to read and gather everything I could about my spiritual practice. I had stacks of books by Scott Cunningham and Gerald Gardner piled next to my bed, the pages dog-eared and stained.

Larry and I would go out into the woods behind the house, barefoot in the dirt, and cast a circle under the sky. I introduced him to Wicca, and he understood it instantly. We were so similar. I was the stronger of the two. Larry was a big, handsome country boy, yet underneath that exterior he was a smart, shy man who could play every instrument he picked up. His main passion was drumming, and he played with several bands upstate. He came out of that whole Skid Row scene.

I became deeply attached to Larry, loved him fiercely, and together we disappeared down the rabbit hole. We funneled through loads of cash. The Doctor tolerated it and financed it. Incredible, I know. Who in their right mind lets a young woman move her boyfriend and two gay friends into their home? But he did. He truly loved me, and I loved him as much as I was capable of at the time. Only now am I appalled by my behavior.

Back then, I was let loose to tear through the streets like a child with zero responsibilities. My only concern was whether the dealer had what I needed. I threw my money at dealers and tried to smother the internal agony that never stopped raging. Pain of childhood abuse and neglect. I needed peace. I needed the Goddess to shine a light on me, and she guided me as much as she could considering my mental state. I didn't understand anything. I was completely fractured, lost in cocaine psychosis.

And yet I'd still light candles, burn sage and frankincense, call the four quarters, and feel something ancient move through me. It was the only time I felt truly clean, truly connected to something bigger than the chaos I was living in. I lived my religion. It's always been who I am.

Wicca gave me a framework for understanding the energy that flows through everything, the cycles of death and rebirth, the balance between light and dark. I believed in the Goddess and the God, in the turning of the Wheel of the Year, in the power of my own will to shape reality. When I was out in nature, surrounded by green and my animals, I felt at peace. The cats wove between my legs during rituals, and Jezebella, my beautiful Rottweiler, lay nearby guarding and watching. Out there, with the earth beneath my feet and the scent of rich soil rising up, I wasn't just some junkie. I was a witch. I was all-powerful.

The contradiction never escaped me. I'd nod out with a needle in my arm one night and wake up the next morning to greet the sunrise, making pentagrams out of twigs and praying to the Goddess. I'd shoot dope and later that same day, cook a stew with herbs, stirring it clockwise for prosperity and protection. Somehow it all made sense to me. The drugs were about escape, about numbing a constant pain. The Craft was about presence, about feeling everything, about claiming my power in a world that tried to take it from me. Both were forms of magick, I guess. One just happened to be killing me.

The Doctor believed he wasn't buying sex or companionship. He thought he was buying the illusion that money can fix something broken. He believed his support and generosity could save me, that enough Valium, a Mercedes, and a house could somehow pull me back from the edge. But addiction doesn't work like that. You can throw all the money in the world into a black hole, and it will swallow it without getting any smaller.

I was a twenty-year-old woman slowly killing herself, childhood trauma chewing through every thought. I needed something, anything, to stop the internal pain I'd carried for as long as I could remember, a pain born from never having real parents. They gave birth to me, but parents they were not. And I hadn't spoken to them in many years. The Doctor's kindness was real, but it was enabling to the highest degree, and the line between love and destruction is often thinner than a needle.

Years later, when I finally found my way to a soft place to land, I understood what The Doctor had been searching for. He wasn't just trying to save me. He was trying to save himself from the sterile predictability of his own life. In caring for someone as chaotically alive as I was, he felt something he'd lost in examining rooms and delivery wards, the electric uncertainty of a life without guarantees. Maybe he saw freedom in me.

But that realization came many years later. For now, we were just two broken people in a beautiful house, pretending that money could heal what only time and difficult choices ever could.

THE SWIMMING POOL INCIDENT

"The measure of intelligence is the ability to change."
— *Albert Einstein*

The Doctor's offer of stability was a retreat where my life, despite the money and supposed safety, remained a chaotic dance with death. Changing locales proved utterly futile; my mind, a stubborn and treacherous landscape, remained unchanged, the sickness festering, turning every waking thought into a relentless hum for the very substance I needed as much as air.

Until the house the doctor has purchased for me, or us, is ready, he's rented one of those newish, sprawling suburban cookie-cutter units. On the plus side, you got access to a nice big swimming pool at the entrance of the estate, surrounded by a lovely, manicured rose garden with flowering shrubbery in full bloom.

I'd planned on sitting poolside, acquiring a blistering Tropicana suntan while nodding out with a frosty vodka lemonade and a copy of *Post Office* by Charles Bukowski, and New Order playing on my CD player. Such was the idyllic dream of suburban loveliness. Unfortunately, before I ever got to sit by that pool, I found myself almost drowning in it.

I knew a smack dealer, Flaco, who had recently set up in a basement apartment at the far end of the complex with his family. As any addict can attest, we can sniff out a bag of dope from across the street in a blinding snowstorm. That's how we met, though it wasn't snowing but raining hard, and I was at a gas station in town.

Maybe it was my charm he sniffed out as I paid for gas, a pack of Newport's, rolling papers, and a

Snowball. I like to peel the marshmallow off, saving it after I devour the chocolate cake inside. Maybe he saw the blood spots on my shirt sleeve or was I emitting a junkie aura? I always thought I could pass, but clearly cracks were beginning to show.

Flaco sauntered over and asked outright if I was "good?" He introduced himself, gave me his pager number, told me to call anytime for girl and boy (coke and dope). A little nervy, but I'm always on the lookout for good drugs, and I thoroughly appreciated this. Sometimes the universe is just looking out for you.

The small-town upstate heroin dealers tacked on a hefty ten-buck surcharge to each normally priced $10 bag. A $10 bag in Manhattan cost $20 upstate. On the other hand, it wasn't my money; it was The Doctor's.

The dope always seemed to run out quickly, but I was a professional and always saved a wake-up. Still, I needed more. In the immortal words of Iggy Pop: I (always) Need More.

I called Flaco, but first I had to withdraw $300 from the bank, which was closed (it was Sunday) and for some reason the ATM was located inside the bank (this was before ATMs were planted on every street). Always an obstacle. Being an active addict is more work than any straight job.

Following a manipulative phone call, I cadged The Doctor into wiring me $350 from his office in Port Jervis to Middletown Western Union, a couple towns away. If you ever want to meet desperate junkies in any American city, spend quality time at your local Western Union.

Behind the scratched, bulletproof window, the Western Union lady (a sizeable woman with a cheeseburger-sized, gold-plated cross around her neck) gave me the side-eye every time she counted out my cash. I'd say, "Thank you," with a delighted smile, because that cash was the next step in the process. Each step brought me closer to God. I mean, heroin. She'd say, "Ah hum," with pursed, glossy lips.

I'd done this same thing three days ago, then again, a few days before that. Who was I kidding? It had been regular for a long while.

Back in my car, using the brand-new portable phone The Doctor bought me (the size of two bricks for those who remember life before pocket computers), I dialed Flaco's number, feeling like a spoiled rich bitch.

"Flaco, hi, yes it's Zoe, can I stop by?" I held my breath and crossed my fingers, waiting for the blessed "OK, come on over."

"Mamma, wha you nee? Youse stoppin' by?" Flaco said in his heavy Hispanic accent.

"I want three albums, two slow ones, and one fast one. I'll be there in five." I'm sure this code wouldn't foil the dumbest of cops, but everyone spoke in record amounts.

Just hearing "come on over" was unquestionably the best news I could hear.

Through watering eyes and wide yawns, I sniffled my way around the winding country roads, driving fast, praying a deer didn't step onto this highway of death. I needed a toilet badly. After the yawns and sniffles came the dire need to poop, then compulsive sneezes. I sneezed nine times in a row (my record was twelve) and swerved to miss an oncoming car. They honked and flipped me off. Fuck 'em.

I was freezing, my face sweating. My legs began to spasm, and I had to punch my thighs to keep from doing an impromptu cancan that would undoubtedly wrap me around one of the 200-year-old oaks lining the road.

Finally, I saw the complex entrance. Adrenaline

flooded my quivering system. I clenched my ass cheeks, my stomach gurgling like a cauldron of lava.

The bright sun was making everyone's day pleasanter, but not mine. It was making my eyes water, and I was beginning to resent it. I wished the sun could make me happy, but no chance. I liked the rain. Dark, menacing skies were comforting, like being tucked into a warm, safe bed.

But I needed to focus. I was almost there. I hit the turn signal, steered my clammy wheel to the left, and in that second, I saw the shimmering pool water out of the corner of my eye. And somehow, what the fuck, the car was heading towards the water. Fast! I felt the small plants and rocks under the carriage, heard those lovely roses brushing my car doors as I veered into the beautiful, calm blue water.

One minute I was driving along, the next I was in a swimming pool, in my Mercedes, just kind of floating. WHAT was happening? How did I get here? This must be a dream, except ouch, fuck! My neck hurt, so it must be real. OH God! NOOOOOO!

I was in total panic mode, gulping chlorine. I looked around to see if anyone was in the pool when I landed in it. Thankfully, no one. I pulled myself out of the open driver's window and doggie-paddled to the side.

And all the while I was thinking, thank God almighty I hadn't copped yet, because I'd die an absolute death if all my drugs got soaked in the swimming pool. Now that's a tragedy.

I was wet and sick and completely stunned. My mind could not comprehend the magnitude of what had happened. So, what did I do? I ran to Flaco's house, leaving a trail of wet footprints from the scene of the crime all the way to his basement apartment.

People stared as I sprinted past them, soaked and sneezing, but no one was running after me. I couldn't bear to look back or think about the destruction I'd caused, starting with that beautiful rose garden. I hated myself all over the place.

"It's me, Zoe," I whispered to the door.

Flaco threw open the door, his large, round hazel eyes getting even bigger. He stared me up and down with his usual smirk-slash-smile. "Damn girl, is it raining out there?"

"Funny! No, it's not raining."

"Den why da fuck youse wet?" he was puzzled.

"You're never gonna believe this," I began, "or maybe you will..."

Not until I heard myself explain and saw Flaco's reaction did I realize how completely insane I sounded.

"WHAT!" His voice came out an octave higher. "Wa you mean you lef your car in da pool, an' ran over here...?"

"Uh, I dunno what happened, it was an accident," I said nervously.

"Girl, you crazy, they gonna be looking for your ass! You gotta get up outta this bitch..." He slapped the dope in my hand. "Take this an' get to getting'. Go on now. You too crazy, London, you just too damn crazy." He smiled.

Some street people called me London because of my accent and hometown. Despite everything, Flaco liked me, and I prayed this mishap wouldn't get me banned from his premium product.

I handed over the $300 and snatched the two bundles and a little party pack of blow. My usual pickup. In the city, this shit would have been extremely rare. Most suppliers stepped on it with crap, ruining God's good drugs until it was nothing but baby laxative and speed. But Flaco's stuff was cut straight off the brick. You could see pure crystals and flecks shining in the lights, and the chemical smell could make you cry with joy.

I called The Doctor from Flaco's and asked him to pick me up. I did not tell him about my unexpected dip in the pool. I awaited sirens any second, terrified I was going to be arrested for leaving the scene of the crime. But really, why limit myself?

In a way, it was like a beautiful art piece, something staged by Chris Burden maybe. My car, resting majestically at the bottom of the pool. Oh my God! What had I done? They'd definitely be looking for me by now.

And yet when The Doctor picked me up, he said nothing about the car in the pool. He just gave me the usual "oh you silly girl" look, for which I was beyond grateful. I didn't want to hear about the awful thing I'd done. I hated myself and what I couldn't seem to control, which was pretty much everything.

I apologized profusely to The Doctor, but it was the law that had my stomach tied in knots. For one second, I thought about taking off, just disappearing. But really, how was that going to work out? I'd spent most of my life moving, changing locations, trying to find a place where I felt safe and comfortable. But what I'm really good at is adapting.

I was summoned to appear in court. Charges included leaving the scene, property damage, reckless driving, and a few other things I've mercifully forgotten. I was absolutely certain I was going away. They must have found syringes and random paraphernalia in my car, and God knows what other druggy detritus.

Thanks to The Doctor's largess, I owned a Wiccan esoteric supply store with a tattooist and body piercer. I also sold rock-n-roll clothing, mainly rubber pants T-shirts, belts, make-up with my Jezebella logo that Larry had designed beautifully. The local warlocks and Wiccans browsed my shop, and I'd amassed a loyal customer base of youngsters wanting edgier stuff to fill their brains with (this was pre-internet).

I named my store Jezebella, after my beloved Rottweiler, located in downtown Middletown between the local police station and a decrepit, hand-job-in-the-back stripper bar called Rudy's. Because sometimes, ladies and gentlemen, life really is perfect.

The town's mayor himself came by to give me a plaque and let me know how delighted he was that my business was such a success. I'd been featured in the local paper, the Middletown Sleepy Tribune, or whatever it was called. I wasn't capable of actually running the day-to-day goings on, so I hired a lovely young girl who was in mortician school, her name was Jen. Larry and I would drop by to grab money and whatever else we wanted on our way to the local dealers in the town.

Chaos ensued over the next few weeks while I waited for my court date. When you're a junkie, chaos is your job, and I'd become good at it. I thought I was living an artistic, exciting, dangerous existence. In reality, my life was a fucking mess that had gotten completely out of control. It always had been, but this was my reality. I saw no way out. I was being buried alive in my addiction.

MY DAY IN COURT

"I recognize in thieves, traitors and murderers, in the ruthless and the cunning, a deep beauty: a sunken beauty. —"Jean Genet

As someone whose life often felt like a series of daring escapes and improbable misadventures, the idea of a simple court date seemed almost quaint. Yet facing a judge for my latest exploit, a spontaneous aquatic parking job that left a rose garden in ruins and my Mercedes a makeshift submarine, held its own unique dread. I'd walked away from plenty of scrapes before, but this time felt different, like the universe was finally calling in some overdue debts.

In the weeks leading up to my court date, I'd convinced myself this was it: the end of my brief experiment with suburban living. I'd seen enough episodes of Night Court to know how these things went. The gavel would fall, the handcuffs would click, and I'd be trading my Frye boots for orange jumpsuits. The Doctor had already started making the phone calls lawyers make when they know their client is fucked, and I'd begun mentally preparing for a very different kind of detox program, courtesy of the state.

My day in court came way too soon. But who really doesn't feel that way when it's their time on the hot seat? Oddly enough, I was simply issued a date. My luck, as ever, was far better than I deserved.

I knew someone who ended up in Rikers for jumping turnstiles in Harlem, and here I was, endangering lives, wiping out rose gardens, and plopping like a one-woman aircraft carrier into a public swimming pool.

Needless to say, I dressed for the occasion. I ironed

a white linen shirt I'd never worn but kept at the back of my closet and paired it with a pleated, knee-length flowered skirt from Neiman Marcus. Again, never worn. It wasn't my style, but it would do for court.

I felt and looked thoroughly unlike myself. My long, dark, wildly thick mane was neatly blown out, as best I could manage. I slipped on my favorite Peter Fox pumps, the only part of my outfit I liked, the only part that looked like me. They were black suede with a rounded toe and a beautiful five-inch flared heel.

I had no idea if I'd be arrested in court on the "leaving the scene" charge, or what the hell else. Just in case, I said my goodbyes to my Rottweiler, all the cats, my best friend Brian, and the Doctor himself. I had no idea if or when I would be coming home again. Of course, Larry accompanied me to court.

It was my first time in a country-style courtroom, but not my first time in front of a judge. I'd had a couple of arrests back in New York City and had spent two or three chilly nights in the Tombs. I mean, who hasn't?

This time in court, I wasn't with a lawyer. I was told to show up, so show up I did, and plead my own case. The courtroom was cold and wood-paneled. After five minutes, I immediately regretted not wearing long johns. The scent of floor polish was strong enough to make your nose hairs waxy. The judge was middle-aged and pleasantly reminded me of Donald Sutherland with dark hair. His face was kind, his voice polite, and he gave the impression that he wasn't your typical overworked, uninterested judge. He wore bifocals low on his nose, and when he spoke, it was with more curiosity than malice.

"Ms. Hansen," he began, "I see here that you're the young lady who drove her car into a swimming pool! I've heard about you." He peered at me over his bifocals, taking me in with a half-grin and a raised left brow.

"Yes, Judge," I replied. I started to say "Your Honor," but caught myself. I never wanted to appear ass-kissing.

"Well, well, well." He looked over to his court officer, who nodded, his thin lips curling into a half-grin. He looked at me, then the floor. The court

officer was a large man, older, maybe fifty years or so, and judging by his appearance, definitely enjoyed a beer or few with the guys. "Yes, Judge," I heard myself say again. This time I lowered my head, fully expecting to hear the amount of damage I'd caused, the expense of towing my car out of the pool (that couldn't have been easy), and all the other dreadfully embarrassing charges they could throw at me. And they wouldn't have been wrong.

I was never a good student, but I could perform when necessary. So, in my best, sharpened British accent, I pleaded my case. Strangely, I didn't need to do much pleading.

Peering over his glasses from the bench, he continued, "So, Ms. Hansen, it says here that you drove your car, a Mercedes 300 SE, into the swimming pool at... where was it? Ah, I see... West View Garden Estate, Middletown, off Route 17... Oh my!" Who doesn't like a gentleman who says "Oh my?" I've always found that remark irresistible in a man of a certain age, and I think they should bring it back.

He chuckled again, and in spite of myself, I thought I liked this man. I raised my head and stared in complete shock and confusion as he began to laugh. Not some polite, affected guffaw, but a full-on belly chuckle, as though he was really enjoying himself. I looked around. Was I missing something here? The judge was looking at me, and what he saw, for whatever reason, amused him.

"Well, Your Honor," (I felt "Your Honor" would

now serve me better. I needed to plead my case, and the judge was acting like some long-lost uncle, for which I was unbelievably thankful) "I'm completely mortified at what I've done and I'm so sorry. I guess I must have taken a wrong turn..."

"I'll say you did... Hahahaha." By now His Honor had removed his bifocals and was wiping his eyes with a hanky. I stood dumbfounded, and now I really didn't know what to think. Was this a joke? A trick? Must be some legalistic fun and games I wasn't aware of. So, I guess I'd go along with it.

Taking their cue from the judge, the other members of the court staff were all half-smiling at me, like we were old friends. Oh no, maybe they'd gotten me confused with someone else. There's no way they could think my colossal accident and destruction amusing, is there?

"All right," the judge continued, "so you make a wrong turn. And then?"

"And then, I realized I was wet... and floating."

"You realized you were wet?" The judge's eyes widened and more chuckles, some guffaws. It's like open mike night at Yuk-Yuk's Comedy Cavern, and somehow, I'm KILLING.

We went on like this, exchanging light banter, until much to my complete and utter disbelief, the judge smiled some more, nudged his glasses up his nose and declared:

"Well, Ms. Hansen, we won't waste any more of your time. I'm sure you're a very busy woman. So go on, you're free to leave... Though I have to say, it's pretty darn funny, and my kids are gonna be over the moon when I tell 'em I met the young lady who drove her Mercedes off the deep end... into the swimming pool, at West View. You know you've become somewhat famous over this whole event."

"I have?" I replied. I'm stunned. Surely this is a

mistake, a joke? What's going on?

And here, you guessed it, the judge erupted into laughter all over again.

This was one of the most entertaining cases that had happened in this courtroom in forever, I'm guessing.

Now actually believing that I had, in fact, gone and done something far more funny than catastrophic, I decided to let go a little and run with it.

"What can I say, Your Honor? That pool looked awfully inviting, and it's so much easier and quite a bit cheaper than going to a car wash."

"A car wash! Ha! That's funny. And she's got that cute British accent too. Okay, Ms. Hansen, Pip Pip! Cheerio! Go on, and get out of here. And have a wonderful day. You've certainly given me one. Okay, buh-bye!"

I've come to find out, certain Americans really enjoy mimicking a British accent, and they often want me to remark on how convincingly British they sound.

And with that, he waved me out of the court. I looked around one more time, just to make sure this was real: could the judge actually be dismissing everything? What about the torn-out flowers and shrubbery I'd destroyed? What about the cost of towing my car out of the pool? That couldn't have been easy. Maybe I could come by and fix the garden. That would have been a great idea, but I knew myself. I'd never show up. But still? No community service? No anything? Apparently not. My case was dismissed, and I was free to go and create more havoc.

MEET ASHLEY

"We are what we pretend to be, so we must be careful what we pretend to be." — *Kurt Vonnegut*

I must introduce you to Ashley, my psycho-kleptomaniac sidekick. There was something about her, a spark of thrill beneath a surface that was, unquestionably, disturbing. And, this being my life, she was a true, hope-to-die dope fiend.

Our story began on the Upper East Side, at a small massage studio on 2nd Avenue and 67th Street where I'd picked up a shift. After a slow workday, Ashley and I arranged to earn some extra money on the Park Avenue South track. I'd not worked the streets of New York before and was eager to learn the nuances that would make the difference between a bust and success.

A couple blocks south, Broadway had, after dark, morphed into a "red light" district. Here, beneath awnings and within shadowy doorways, one might find a higher caliber of working woman. A glimmer of beauty and excitement, caught under a street lamp, then, in a flash, she was gone. These women generally weren't drug users, and if they were, they maintained well. With styled hair, professional makeup, and expensive clothing, they commanded the maximum prices. Some were simply mirroring our own predicament: attempting to snag a few punters before calling it a night, a necessary scramble after a financially slow day at the studio. I needed cash as much as air to breath. It was the relentless, gnawing hunger of the heroin addict.

My teacher was Ashley. I trailed her, a moth drawn to a chaotic flame, intrigued, yet cautious, and somewhat amused by my new friend.

Under the awning of the Oak Room bar in the Plaza Hotel on Central Park South, two very young, possibly Russian, blond working women stood, making little pretense of discretion with the trick they were attempting to lure. One eventually disappeared into the Plaza Hotel with a man, while the other remained, subtly gesturing to a black BMW across the street: their pimp, or driver presumably.

We didn't have to venture into the bar that night. It took less than five minutes before we reeled in a shy Asian man loitering outside. He sported suede Ferragamo loafers, a gold Omega watch, and a simple yet classic dark grey cashmere sweater. It's part of my job to note such accessories; they offer an indication of what price point might be acceptable. What sum would he concede? What precise figure would justify the services we were about to render?

He appeared shy and a touch embarrassed by Ashley, struggling even to meet her gaze. Perhaps it was her heavy false lashes, or the overly frosted pink lips, or the splotchy tan. Who could say, she quickly quoted him: two hundred dollars to see her, and she'd "throw me in" for an additional one-fifty. But for the "cool price" of four hundred, he'd get a bi-show and two hot women! How, she challenged, could he possibly resist? I listened in silent awe, impressed by her sheer, unadulterated gall.

To be fair, I didn't think he was terribly interested in the bi-show. That's the thing about this business: you must know your audience. Yet Ashley, with her relentless patter of "double talk" and supposed "discounts", somehow managed to hook him for the full four hundred dollars, reeling us both into the date. To say I was uncomfortable with the whole transaction would be a gross understatement. The man had clearly wanted to see me, attempting to politely articulate his disinterest in Ashley, but she simply feigned deafness. She persisted with her double talk, and before the shy man knew what was happening, the three of us were ascending to his fifth-floor room. I was in awe of Ashley's audacity, and I must admit, I kinda liked it.

I fully intended to give the man his full hour. I felt we'd bamboozled him, and he seemed to be going along with the entire spectacle merely to be a good sport.

Ashley and I launched into the main attraction, which was a "Show," our sister-lesbo performance, usually a best-seller. Most men can't get enough of two women going at it, and it was my job to provide the entertainment, for a price.

But he was uninterested, politely edging towards me, a subtle pursuit Ashley swiftly rebuffed. He then asked us both to simply lie down beside him, to merely be there, quietly. Ashley and I exchanged quizzical glances, and I had to stifle giggles as I lay my head down, the man nestled between us, Ashley making funny faces trying to make me laugh.

Ashley was not one for wasting time. She worked fast. Everyone has their own style and method they feel comfortable with. Me, I like to begin with a sensual massage and build to the main event, which may or may not be sex.

But today, after a mere thirty seconds laying on the bed, Ashley sprung up, straddled his thighs, and began to jerk him off, with the occasional dirty words thrown in, which I knew he didn't care for. I cringed. The client, who, quite frankly, seemed more embarrassed by the entire situation, was clearly having second thoughts about having invited two hookers up to his room at The Plaza Hotel. He came quickly, eager to hide his face in a veil of shame. We collected our four hundred dollars and split.

And even though working with Ashley had been

rather uncomfortable, and embarrassing, I had to hand it to her: she was a force of nature. As partners, I believed we could make bank together. Or so I thought.

A smug smile plastered on my face as I confidently strode through the beautiful, if slightly dusty and a tad shabby in corners, old Plaza Hotel, back out onto Central Park South. We strolled past the two young women still working the bar; they stared at us as we hailed a cab and headed downtown to "cop." We didn't think we were slick; we knew we were. And in that moment, I was on top of the world.

Plucking a man off the street and netting four hundred bucks' cash in twenty minutes was profoundly confidence-building, and it made me crave more.

Ashley and I soon began running together, getting high together, and, theoretically, keeping an eye on each other's backs. But I'm getting ahead of myself...

When Ashley and I met, the connection was instant. Always in need of another "cool chick" to generate income with, Ashley immediately recognized the amplified potential of a team effort. Junkies, to put it plainly, possess an uncanny, almost telepathic ability to sense one another. Seriously. Airdrop me into a strange city, and I can pinpoint the DDM (Designated Drug Market) in under a minute. As the saying goes, a dope fiend could spot another, even if both were albino, lost in a blizzard. Or something... Call it narcotic sonar. It's a gift.

Ashley had been in the game for a while, usually operating solo. I figured I might learn a thing or two. And she certainly needed me as an accomplice, for crime is undeniably easier with a partner.

We placed an ad in New York Magazine, buried in the back section, the "adult" pages offering massages, escorts, dominatrixes, and trans women for hire.

Sexual services, of course, were merely implied, "wink wink." Ashley, naturally, included a photograph of herself, looking as much like a big-chested Pam Anderson knock-off as humanly possible. It drew a steady trickle of "tricks." I, meanwhile, came in as the "add-on." Ashley possessed a remarkable knack for convincing her clients to indulge in the "two-for- one special," which simply meant two women at once, with the promise of a "bi-show" for a generous tip. They never turned down the offer, and we proceeded to work remarkably well together. Our primary haunts became the Hilton on Sixth Avenue and the Hyatt Hotel bar next to Grand Central Station, where we managed to book a slew of famous sports players. From Barry Bonds to Charles Barkley. At the time, I had no clue who they were, as I followed no sports of any kind. It was only later, seeing Bonds' star rise in the media, that I recognized him as the cool, young man who'd booked me on multiple occasions. Bonds, incidentally, did not like Ashley at all, and that messed with her head, and I was okay with that.

The fact that I knew nothing about baseball, or any other kind of ball, seemed to genuinely tickle Barry. Which I understand. But even with a gun to my head, I couldn't have told you the number on his jersey. And, for the record, all that talk about steroids shrinking the equipment... Not so much. He was just fun. To me, they were simply polite, cool guys, clearly on their way to stardom, even then. Barry wore a small gold chain around his neck with his name on it: "Barry Bonds" in shimmering gold. But being me, when I glanced at it, I thought it read "Gary U.S. Bonds," a name familiar if you know your R&B. (I should mention, I was diagnosed with dyslexia as an adult, which finally answered so many lingering questions about my childhood struggles with spelling and reading, despite my love for books.) It was a short-lived romance, Barry's and mine, but whenever he was in New York, I'd receive a call to his hotel room. And between us, there was, undeniably, a kind of mutual respect.

Ashley resembled Dolly Parton, had Dolly Parton passed out on Xanax in a tornado and woken up a day later behind a party supply store. Yet, in Ashley's mind, she was nothing less than Pam Anderson's doppelganger. She was, she believed (with enough drugs coursing through her veins), Pamela Anderson.

Ashley invested in double-D silicone implants, a surgical decision that left her with a nasty scar around each nipple. But all the "girlies" were getting them; I considered it for a minute but decided to wait. Ashley also habitually slept in her Mediterranean blue contact lenses, a practice that frequently resulted in a nasty pink eye, forcing her to remove one blue contact and reveal her own unremarkable brown peeper. She never removed both, just the offending, dripping blue/pink eyeball. I'd have removed both, but that's our Ashley.

The real trouble, however, was Ashley's insistence that her deep-lagoon-blue eyeballs were, in fact, hereditary, passed down from her dear, sweet grandmother. Clients, I think, were often too embarrassed to challenge her ridiculous lies. Her stories had long ceased being mere fibs; they were now straight-up lies layered upon delusion, upon sheer, diabolical junkie shit. She was also completely blind, a fact I, for some reason, found charming. Perhaps it was the only truly authentic thing about Ashley. And she couldn't possibly navigate life with the large "Italian honker" she'd also inherited from that same grandmother, so she had it shaved down. And it didn't look half bad.

(I, incidentally, was born with a button nose, also inherited from my grandmother on my British side, and have been accused of having a nose job on many occasions. I broke it a few years ago, leaving a slight bump; it shows character, I'm told.)

Ashley wouldn't have been the quintessential 1990s glamour chick she strived so hard to be without the home bleach job. She always missed patches in the back, but it was the early '90s, and the towering front-tease "puff" was everything. The flat back of one's hair seemed easily forgotten. Another glaring facet of Ashley's appearance was her permanently coffee-stained palms. She'd slather Jergens self-tanner foam over her body, always patchy, and invariably forgot to wash her hands afterward. So, her palms remained a deep, reddish-brown; it looked positively bizarre.

Did I mention Ashley told everyone she was a Playboy centerfold? An embellishment that wisely allowed her to tack a few hundred bucks onto her hourly fee. Of course, Ashley was never a centerfold, or even a model. She'd had modeling cards fabricated, complete with her measurements, weight, foot size, and a few thumbnail snapshots, creating the illusion for the untrained eye that she was a professional model and Playboy cover girl. "Delusion is the key to happiness," a wise man once said. And why the heck not. Had the Kardashians graced the cultural landscape back then, Ashley would most likely have emulated Kim. But in the '90s, Pamela Anderson reigned, and Ashley did her damnedest to appear as anything but herself.

Did I mention she was an incredible kleptomaniac? Truly gifted.

We "went shopping" regularly. And by shopping, Ashley meant simply taking whatever she desired off the racks and waltzing out with it. Actually, paying for anything was decidedly not on the menu. One weekday afternoon, we strolled into Chanel on Fifth Avenue. Ashley swiped a beautiful, very expensive little black suit. And I saw nothing. She'd taken a few suits into the dressing room and, with sleight of hand, simply snatched one. She was that good. And honestly, I was profoundly jealous of her collection of luxury stolen goods. I simply didn't possess the nerve, or the stomach for the humiliation of being caught stealing. I'd rather pay.

Ashley could have a purse overflowing with C-notes and still boost whatever caught her eye. I don't believe she ever walked into a store without lifting something, anything. Perhaps she felt the world owed it to her. There was this one time, uptown on busy 57th Street. Ashley and I ambled into a Victoria's Secret dressing room, loaded down with an impressive haul of lingerie. As I waited, I distinctly heard the sharp snap of anti-theft tags being torn off, most likely with her teeth, then spat onto the dressing room floor. Sometimes items got ripped in the process, but a little tear never bothered Ashley. In fact, I later noticed that all of Ashley's expensive silk blouses bore a tell-tale rip at the neck, precisely where the tag used to be. One might think she'd have swiped one of those little machines designed to remove tags without destroying the clothes, but perhaps I'm getting too innovative. "I can open beer bottles with my teeth," she once informed me. Ashley was one of those women who opened everything with her teeth. It's a type.

Then she'd gather the tags, tucking them discreetly into the sleeve of her fake fur jacket. Then, she'd breeze out of the dressing room, twenty bras and countless pairs of undies now adorning her body, under her clothing. We needed a spot to dump the evidence, so I suggested she subtly open an underwear drawer on the floor, allowing the tags to slide out of her sleeve and vanish within. Brilliant, right? Five minutes later, a shop assistant suddenly discovered the incriminating pile of ripped-off tags in the same underwear drawer. A flurry of store activity erupted, and security was notified via loudspeaker to shut the front entrance. Ashley had genuinely grown nervous. We made a quick dash for the exit, slipping out just as the security gates were clanking shut behind us! We raced down Fifth Avenue, each arm laden with shopping bags, and collapsed in a heap of relief and laughter around the corner on Broadway. There is, truly, nothing more exhilarating in this world than getting over.

Another bizarre observation: she didn't actually need any of the items she stole. In fact, she rarely even wore much of it. She simply hoarded everything, all of it pilfered. There must be some profoundly compelling psychological reason behind her kleptomania, one I'll likely never uncover.

Ashley's small walk-up apartment on Second Avenue and Twenty-Ninth Street could have been an adorable little home for someone else. But Ashley had transformed it into a squalid mess: mountains of clothing, boxes of outgrown toys for her son, a truly heartbreaking sight. It showed that she had once tried to be a good mother, who loved her child, but as an addict, she was utterly incapable of providing a safe, secure environment. Her four-poster metal bed consumed the majority of her bedroom. What started as a lovely space was now obscured by rows of stolen clothes hanging around the frame. One would have to peel away an area just to climb into the bed, a bed that may or may not have a hypodermic needle randomly stuck in its bedding. She invited her clients into that bedroom, all the while her young son, Hunter, sat in his tiny room right next to hers. She'd found him peering through the keyhole into her room, spying on his mother. It was a chaotic, profoundly distressing way for a child to be raised.

Around this time, I stumbled upon some photos of

Ashley in seductive poses, framed poorly, out of focus. When I inquired about them, she casually explained that Hunter had taken them. She was trying to save money, having her seven-year-old snap her "whoring pics" for advertising! I had nothing to say. She never listened to my concerns for Hunter anyway, and she was right: I am not a mother; I cannot truly judge.

Yet, lacking any viable options, and driven by my gnawing conscience for her son, I called social services. What Ashley was doing to this kid wasn't right. Although she loved him dearly, she was not mentally capable of providing for him. He was seeing and hearing things a seven-year-old should never witness, and it was only a matter of time before something truly awful happened. I knew I'd never forgive myself if I didn't attempt to intervene in the best way, I knew possible.

There is no "best way," and I was undeniably putting myself in danger. But the situation I laid out was not enough for the agency to rescue her child. I happened to be there, in her apartment, when a social worker knocked on the door. He merely peeked his head inside, and Ashley, looking directly at me, declared, "I've no idea why anyone would call social services on me..." I returned her gaze with my best blank stare. I felt terrible for her son, and the social worker simply left without so much as walking into the seedy apartment.

After that first nonsensical visit, it became painfully clear that social services weren't going to help him. This was a dire situation. Yet, this particular social worker was clearly unfamiliar with the high-tier manipulation Ashley had perfected for unaware men. He was exactly the type to see the image she wanted him to see. He, a slight man of Hispanic descent, saw a large-breasted, pretty white woman. She couldn't possibly be responsible for the child neglect allegations, could she? No, not this pretty white woman, with deep, bloody tracks on the backs of her hands and one tearing, pink eye from a raging infection.

You see, a savvy social worker would have known exactly what was going on. And I'm still amazed that man walked away from the apartment without so much as asking to meet the child involved. I called again and received the same dismissive response. Hunter's behavior grew increasingly uncontrollable, and for a young, strung-out, mentally unbalanced, undiagnosed, compulsively thieving, and prostituting mother, it was, understandably, all too much. At the time, for a fleeting moment, I thought Ashley was incredibly cool. But it didn't take long before her bizarre, messy, sociopathic personality began to seep through every crack. Ashley retreated further into her madness, and for whatever psycho- emotional reasons, she became nastier, stranger, and there's no other word for it, even more diabolical.

STRANDED IN TRUMP'S CASINO

"While anti-sex work feminists see trading sex as the ultimate concession to patriarchy, I see it as a refusal."
— *Matilda Bickers*

One chilly late September evening, Ashley, with her singular brand of persuasion, convinced me to accompany her to Atlantic City. She'd booked a small bachelor party there, and having survived a couple of these events with her before, I assumed this one would be much the same. She managed the incidentals, as it was her client, and I was still allowing Ashley to lead the way, still fantasizing she was the sophisticated whore she so strenuously strove to be.

I braced myself for the usual tableau: a cluster of young, straight, white, drunk dudes, living their "best life," getting loaded and serviced by two hookers before the inevitable ring ceremony the next day. Bachelor parties were, to me, a dreadfully uncomfortable and uncouth purgatory, yet the cash made the ordeal worthwhile.

There was, mercifully, only one time it ever happened: a young man, well, late twenties, farted as I was blowing him. The repulsion was visceral. I sprang up, a revolted grimace contorting my face, nose scrunched in disgust, and promptly declared myself done with all of them. I gagged, attempting to purge the beer-jock odor from my delicate nostrils, informing them their friend had "farted" while getting blown. It was, in hindsight, somewhat funny, and his friends' laughter at his expense was precisely my point. Still, I wanted to throw up. And to this day, I can still conjure the particularly gruesome scent of that beer-jock fart.

The plan was simple: Ashley and I would take a taxi (a concept I now know sounds absurd, but that was our reality) to Atlantic City. There, we would meet

up with a group of young "suits" eager to perform the traditional male ritual before marriage. They'd get loaded as if preparing for war, and apparently, all wanted to be "fucked" by a prostitute. You know... tradition. Ashley insisted on making all arrangements, likely to skim extra cash without my knowledge. I put nothing past this woman. My sole responsibility was to simply show up.

So, we arrived in Atlantic City, only to discover Ashley had somehow forgotten the address. She hadn't the client's name, his hotel, or his phone number. (This was pre-cell phone, for whatever difference that made. No amount of technology can insulate a situation from a drug-addled maniac's sabotage, but I digress.) Still, Ashley seethed, silently, intensely. She would have loved to blame me, but I'd had absolutely nothing to do with the arrangements, and she knew it.

My survival instincts, honed by years of precarious existence, kicked in. I quickly concocted a plan. It was basic, obvious, and born of desperation: we would simply pluck a couple of punters off the casino floor. This, after all, was what we did. We were cashless and certainly couldn't return home empty-handed. Plus, we needed cab fare. What kind of whore couldn't pull a trick in a casino? This was like shooting dead fish in a barrel.

And so, there we stood, predatory gazes sweeping the casino floor, surrounded by a gruesome buffet of vulgar gold and red, permeated by the rank, warming pan waft of fish. And, inexplicably, enough fruit salad spilling from silver tureens to feed a family of gorillas. The air hummed with a cacophony of sounds: bells ringing, coins dropping, canned music emanating from one-armed bandits. Triumphant congratulations tinkled out to winners and losers, because everyone's a winner at Trump's casino. You know, the monstrosity he constructed, where he famously refused to pay the locals who built the god-awful spectacle in the first place, forcing them into bankruptcy after his arrival. Fast forward three decades, he would, believe it or not (and you can't, can you?) do precisely the same to our fine country. But I'm getting far too ahead of myself; it's still only the 1990s, and conspiracy theorists are still interesting and quirky, not outright purveyors of lies and maniacal misogyny. And I certainly don't want to give away what's going to happen to us all. I cast my gaze around the casino, feeling an immense headache bloom from the assault on my senses.

Ashley and I sauntered around the poker tables, observing groups of older men hunched over cards and bourbon, oblivious to our presence. Beside them, testosterone-dripping young Wall Street geeks plied their luck at craps. We didn't even glance at the younger men. I prefer them older, and by definition, richer. But at that moment, we were in desperate need of just one punter, simply one, so we could afford a damn cab home. I watched small fortunes get sucked into that craps table. Does anyone actually win at craps? We ambled around, slowing by each group of male gamblers, waiting for that specific look, when eyes lock and you know precisely what they want. And what they want is you. They don't want to date you, or take you out. These men pay you to leave. And that dynamic suited me just fine.

Where to begin? The night in question, as they say, became a relentless ricochet from one disaster to another. Allow me to paint a picture for those of you who are visually oriented. Ashley, with her enormous silicone breasts, slinked around in a full-length, pink rubber, skin-tight dress. (From, if you'll pardon the plug, my now-closed rubber fetish-wear store, Jezebella, on 7th St between A and B.) When I moved back to the East Village from upstate New York, I opened my second clothing store. The first Jezebella shop upstate had been really successful. I sold esoteric books, crystals, Wiccan supplies, and rubber and leather fetish gear, rock 'n' roll clothing, jewelry and posters. My clientele included musicians, artists, strippers, and the merely curious who took a wrong turn at Saint Marks Place.

So, Ashley had acquired a pink, floor-length rubber dress from Jezebella. Well, she never actually paid me for the $190 dress, and she'd decided this bachelor party would be the perfect time to premiere it. Did I mention Ashley is fiercely competitive with all females, and utterly convinced every male wants her? Which is fine by me, and I'm certain there was a time she was a genuine head-turner.

The pretend-Playboy story always impressed men. I don't think any of the clients who knew she was lying cared either way. Because they could now brag to their bros that they fucked an actual centerfold! Not a Hustler skank, but a real, smooth, golden-hour Playboy model. Isn't that every male's dream, and some females? For these guys, it was money well spent. No one ever asked for confirmation of the Playboy centerfold story.

On this particular evening, I was wearing a body-hugging, fire-engine red dress that hit just below my knees, held up by spaghetti straps. The dress was by Patricia Fields, and my coat was Chanel (a gift from my father for my 16th birthday.) We'd been through a lot together; that coat has met a lot of famous people. I always wore Chanel when I booked high-class escorting jobs. So, despite our desperate circumstances, I tried to cling to the patina of class.

With everything against us, and the evening rapidly escalating into a stress-fest of tremendous proportions, within three minutes of wandering the casino floor, scoping out possible clients, Ashley's skin-tight pink rubber dress split all the way up one side, to her waist! This is the downside of rubber clothing. One minute you look like a pink Barbie doll, sort of. The next, the rubber splits and tears, and your entire ass is on blast. (Nobody wears panties under rubber, so it's pretty much nature's way, under there.) Perhaps this is why rubber went out of style. Except, of course, for the die-hard fetishists. So now, pardon the sidebar, Ashley's entire left side was exposed. Luckily, she had worn one of her fake furs (she must have shoplifted half a dozen of them), the ones where the fur looked like it was shaved off a teddy bear and pasted back on a coat.

We were stranded. Two drug habits, no money, and a room full of potential tricks. This was precisely one of those situations where you must access your sense of humor. Not something I was capable of at the time. In the rearview mirror, however, it's about surviving, and it certainly feels like the setup for a great, darkly funny movie.

ENTER: Ashley and Zoe stride confidently down the steps into the main floor of Trump's gaudy golden casino. Camera pans to Zoe, in a red spaghetti-strap dress, Chanel coat, long black hair blown out into a full Jaclyn Smith, both looking every inch the high-class hookers. Camera pans to Ashley, who takes a step down the stairway entrance, as her rubber dress splits up to her crotch! ... and the rest of the story unfolds...

We gazed at the room, inspiration striking simultaneously. We both spotted a pair of ripe craps players. One young, one younger. They must be brothers, and the younger one had just won a bit of cash, eager for the world to know. Not exactly a sophisticated duo. But what the hell. We weren't here to discuss Proust.

As if rehearsed, Ashley and I both smiled at the dice players. They smiled back. Meanwhile, Ashley struggled to make the massive rip in her dress appear as some kind of cutting-edge trend. She half-covered it, half-flaunted it. I went with my best Veronica Lake come-hither smile from beneath my corner part.

The two brothers strode over to us, magnetized and curious; they introduced themselves. We inquired (as one does) if they wanted "company." The older brother said yes, and then, attempting sophistication, "how much?"

Ashley replied that it would be two-fifty for her. "But," she blurted, as if the thought had just occurred to her, "you guys are so handsome, you can get both of us for three-fifty." My girl went for the hard sell. She lowered her voice to a smoky Newport purr and leaned in close to little brother. "Baby, you get two hot pussies for the price of one, and I know you want to see me go down on my sister."

"Your sister?" big bro echoed, somewhat skeptically.

"Oh yeah, baby." Ashley hooked her finger in his loosened tie and pulled him closer. "She is my real sister. But, I'm the younger one, the baby!" The nerve of her! Ashley winked at me.

"Umm, wow," says Junior. "Let me think about that for a minute." "Well, hurry up," I snapped, playing good bitch, bad bitch, "we have an appointment in an hour." I fibbed. We had nothing to lose. Ashley shot me a sharp glare. She preferred to be the one to make the deal. But since she's the one who'd gotten us into this calamity, I decided she'd forfeited the right to decide anything.

The two men, we learned their names were Ari and Ali, exchanged glances, mumbling to each other.

When they finally nodded, agreeing to Ashley's $350 two-for-one deal, we wasted no time following them up to their room. All I could think about was securing a one-way ticket out of this day of hell I'd seemed to have walked right into.

When we stepped off the elevator onto their floor, we found ourselves in a rather eerie, winding labyrinth of corridors. They were hushed and stale-smelling, a bizarre combo of sour laundry and strong cleaning products. The air felt greasy, and the awful waft of fish, or possibly fried onions, permeated everything. In the room, I immediately noticed the stained-in-patches popcorn ceiling and hideously patterned bedspread. Wait, was the carpet damp? I knew what we were doing was extremely risky. But as Hyman Roth once said, "this is the business we've chosen," this is the life we lead. There will be times when you know you've escaped within an inch of your life. And times, it's bound to happen, when you don't escape at all. But right now, we had no option. This was it. Our mission was to overwhelm them with tits and pussy.

Ashley always rushed her sessions, which spoke volumes about how she felt about what she did. I don't think she knew how she felt about prostitution, or anything else going on in her tumultuous daily life.

I'd managed many "double sessions" before, which basically meant the client wanted to see two women go down on each other, otherwise known as a "bi-show." With some well-placed long hair, you can make a man believe what he wants to believe. Having been sent to boarding school at the ripe old age of twelve, I wasn't as shy as some ladies who hadn't grown up around a lot of females. It's the silent communication and funny looks from your session partner that make it an easy, and usually quick and humorous, few hundred bucks.

We began our double session. I was attempting to

waste a little time, giving the younger guy my famous gentle, teasing massage, but Ashley went straight for his junk. The other guy pulled his semi-hard dick out and stuck it in Ashley's face. She didn't mind doing two guys at once; I think she preferred it. She always closed her eyes and felt her way through the session, likely her way of dissociating. But, as long as she didn't start with those obscenely loud, porno-inspired, orgasmic moans and groans, it was so cringy.

Ashley wasn't great at subtlety. Her need to rush through sessions always made me uncomfortable. If a client so much as touched her vagina, she'd promptly fake a wild, porno-type orgasm. It was ridiculous, but some men did believe it.

So, here's the picture. Two queen-sized beds, covered in a typically hideous, polyester, wildly disorganized patterned comforter. God knows what human seepage had squirted across this poly-blend, but take it from me: don't touch the bedspread in any hotel.

Ashley collected our $350 and promptly stashed it. I then watched as she slowly peeled off the ripped rubber party dress, inside out, giving us a full view of the now sweating, blotchy orange-brown color she'd covered her body in. Except, she couldn't reach her back, and it was completely white.

Ashley wasted not a moment, going straight in, by aggressively jerking off the older of the two's junk. She then quickly switched to blowing him, as I simultaneously gave the other guy a hand job; he was playing with Ashley's vagina. As stated previously, Ashley was a connoisseur of sexual performance theatrics. She mimicked every porno face and sound she thought men wanted, but she dialed it up to an eleven. I found it the most cringe thing she did in session. Although I'm sure there are men who appreciated her acting abilities, and it made them feel like the He-man stud they all want to be. But those who saw through it, I felt their pain. It was kind of difficult to think anyone could be that naïve regarding women's bodies and sex.

I watched Ari push Ashley's head away when she tried blowing him. So, she got on top of him and thrust her massive bag of boobs into his open mouth, practically suffocating him. His round, dark eyes widened, and a look of fear as his head disappeared into her chest. I had to hide my natural reaction to burst out laughing, and took a moment to collect myself, with my head turned away, before that hysterical laughter began. It's one of the things about doing "doubles" I enjoyed. There's always a moment when you lock eyes with your double partner and have to stifle infectious giggles. Maybe it's nerves, but mainly because the whole scene is actually outrageously funny to me, and made more comedic by the amount of cash we are making for this hour.

I could see his matchstick-like legs and feet, still in his white socks, moving around, his toes curling up, as his penis stuck straight up. And an odd fact is that ninety-nine percent of men kept their socks on while having some form of sexual contact. They could be butt-ass naked, but the socks are stayin'!

Then Ali, or was it Ari? asked to see Ashley and I kiss. I've kissed women before, that wasn't an issue, it was Ashley.

"Oh, honey, I'm sorry, but I don't kiss my sister. Ew, that's gross," I said.

"Aw come on, I wanna see you kiss your sister... down there." He pointed to my vagina.

"Down where?" I teased, rolling my eyes out of sight. I knew what he wanted, but sometimes I enjoyed making them squirm.

Ashley and I went straight into our rehearsed, and performed, girl-on-girl action. I lay down, staring at the dusty ceiling, as one fly buzzed around my head. Ashley hovered over me, posing and stretching her body, as though she was warming up for a yoga class. Sticking out her butt, and arching her back with her pouty frosted pink lips and come-hither eyes. Then in a professional move, Ashley flipped her hair over my crotch, making it impossible for the viewer to see exactly what's going on, while incorporating her moans and yoga stretches in slow motion. I wriggled around copying Ashley's exaggerated throws of ecstasy, with one eye slightly open, while our two men of the hour watched in awe. It was an awkward moment of bodies doing things to other people's bodies.

I was amazed at how smoothly this massive fuck-up was working out, when the younger guy, Ali, suddenly accused Ashley of robbing him! Jesus! I knew Ashley was completely untrustworthy, but I never thought she'd steal from a trick without telling me. Then again, this is Ashley. Why should anything surprise me?

A colossal argument broke out. Junior turned nasty, and quickly. He sported a faint, silky stretch of lip fuzz that had not quite made it to a real mustache. I couldn't stop staring at the way his nose almost touched his top lip when he got truly furious. It's terrifying how he transformed from a normal, relatively nice man to a totally crazed, if slightly effeminate, maniac, screaming at Ashley, calling her every name he could conjure in English and Arabic. Ashley, for her part, was not unfamiliar with this reaction. I'd seen her deal with confrontations, not unlike this one, on more than a few occasions. And somehow, she always wriggled out of the most awkward accusations, relatively unscathed.

I was two seconds from peeing with terror. But I knew I wanted to make it from this fucked-up casino back to Manhattan. I just had to get out of here in one piece. And, note to self, find a more reliable partner. Or at least one who was not like Ashley. Everything that appeared promising about her dissolved into a mess of lies and a slew of excessive drama, invariably ending in us running from something or someone.

Ali demanded that we empty our bags and allow him to search our pockets for the money he swore Ashley had stolen from him. Unspoken, of course, was the nagging fact that the irate brother had ejaculated about three seconds after Ashley pulled down his zipper. No need to mention that. However, sometimes men will want their money back after a premature ejack. But I don't do refunds.

I kept my eyes glued to Ashley, scoping for any signs she might have robbed the guy. But I couldn't tell; she was too good a sociopath. I didn't think she really did steal from him, but who knows. I know nothing; heck, she might have lifted their passports. That is absolutely Ashley's behavior: she takes things that she can't really do much with. She's a kind of hoarder-kleptomaniac.

As Ali or Ari screamed insults at Ashley, the object of his wrath sat on the floor, nonchalantly putting her stuff back into her cluttered handbag, a perverse little half-smile plastered on her smeared pink lips. There was always a lot of junk in Ashley's bag. Random items she'd taken from God knows where: Hilton hotel pens, a notepad from the Plaza, an old-fashioned front desk bell from wherever, and, how handy is this, a RESERVED table sign! You never know when Ashley needed to pretend a table was reserved for her. But hey, look at this: here came a half-dozen bottles of used nail polish she must have lifted when we'd gotten a manicure the day before. The thing is, she didn't need any of the bottles of polish, as she always got her nails painted at the salon.

Again, random junk she didn't need.

As all this transpired, Ari had been standing in front of the door, screaming at a vein-popping volume that he was calling the cops. He wasn't letting us out of the hotel room, and I was beginning to sweat. It was a cacophony of frantic screaming from them, and I was just looking for any way out of this hellish mess. I was getting out of that room, now! While these two were screaming over each other, I seized the moment, when Ari was slightly distracted by Ali, to lunge towards the door handle and yank it open. Before these two guys understood what was happening, I was out the door, with Ashley scrambling behind me. We darted down the long, dark, stale-smelling hall, as the two guys yelled after us into the totally empty corridor. "They robbed me, the fucking whores robbed me! Police, police, get the whores!" Perhaps they'd watched too many American TV shows and anticipated the cops would automatically show up, chasing after us.

Ali, the screamer, hadn't put his pants back on yet. And Ashley, ever the schemer, snatched them from over a chair, before flying out the door, leaving them both standing in the hall yelling, to absolutely no avail. Which was a bit concerning, that not one hotel employee, or anyone for that matter, cared less about two men yelling at the top of their lungs.

I guess this was not uncommon in a Trump casino. In fact, of course it isn't.

The whore Gods were with us, and the elevator door was open, as if waiting. We ducked in, panting, Ashley coughing her perpetual smoker's hack. I'm trying to remain calm and not draw any attention to ourselves.

She wobbled around in her already trashed YSL heels that she'd swiped last week in Bergdorf's, and wore them to death. So, they were scratched, and the heel was definitely going to break, probably before the end of this remarkably catastrophic "everything gone wrong day."

In the elevator I asked, "What the fuck was that? Did you take his wallet?"

"I didn't, really I didn't." She swore on her son, again. Either way, I was done. This was what I meant about Ashley being dangerous. This wasn't out of the ordinary for a day in the life of Ashley, but I just couldn't hang around for much more of it. It wasn't really worth the trouble financially, to have a partner who's so, so, what's the word... totally balls-to-the-wall, off-the-charts frightening. She's also the first actual true sociopath I've encountered.

"What are you going to do with his pants?" I said, looking at the beige Dockers wrapped up in a ball under her arm.

"I dunno, toss them out..." she said.

"Great plan." I sarcastically rolled my eyes to no one but myself. I actually thought it kind of funny that she'd taken his pants at the last second. And to hell with them. I'll never know if she did steal his wallet, but either way, we got the cash to get home.

By the time we made it into a cab and back to Manhattan, neither of us were laughing. In fact, we weren't even speaking. We were exhausted, and it was a long, tense, three-hour cab ride back home.

Daylight was just breaking through, as our cab shot out of the Lincoln Tunnel and across 42nd Street. Fiery golden hues crept up over the morning horizon, casting long shadows through the city's streets. The morning dew, the early city workers, and the birds were singing the blues. I was drained and took a moment to view the city without my own distractions. Finally, we were back home.

THE BACK ROOM AT JEZEBELLA

"One of the most vital ways we sustain ourselves is by building communities of resistance, places where we are not alone." — *bell hooks*

There's a persistent fantasy about sex work, perpetuated mostly by people who've never done it, that it exists in some singular dimension. Penetration, payment, exit. Rinse, repeat. Nothing could be further from the truth.

The work spans from the brutally transactional to the oddly tender, from degradation to worship, from clients who want to dominate to those who beg to submit. The ability to move fluidly across this spectrum, that was the skill that separated the professionals from the amateurs. Let me show you what I mean.

There was one time I conducted a quick S&M session in the back room of Jezebella, my rubber fetish-wear store on 7th Street. A rotund man, approximately thirty-five, clean-shaven with a thick head of dark curly hair, had ambled into the shop. He purchased a cat-o'-nine-tails, a leather mask with a zippered mouth, some Dragon's Blood, and Hecate incense. We made polite small talk while I rang up his items. Trusting my gut, I boldly asked him if he wanted to test that whip in the back room. He nodded, eyes wide, now glistening with sexual anticipation, and lowered his head into the correct slave posture. I had unearthed my dominant side since breaking into the world of prostitution, and these men were all too happy to book me for an exclusive session. It's another type, of which I am apparently one.

I didn't have to ask him; I simply charged his credit

card an extra $150 and pushed the slip towards him to sign, which he did hastily. I then led him in silence to the small back room. It was tight in there, just enough space for shop storage and a makeshift

kitchen. But we could make it work. I've found that clients couldn't care less where the sex, or fetish act takes place, just as long as it does take place.

I ordered him onto his knees and gave him a light lashing with his new whip. I lacked the necessary room for the full flogging he craved but didn't quite deserve. So, I blindfolded him and left the room to pee, ensuring he could hear me. I returned, feigning forgetfulness of his presence, and handcuffed his hands behind his back. Whispering sharply into his ears, "What an undeserving, pathetically lame little fuck slave you are. Not even worth my time." And I left again, to attend to customers in the front of the shop. I came back ten minutes later, unlocked the cuffs and removed his blindfold, then shoved a toilet brush into his face. I leaned down and spat out my words in a sharp whisper into each ear: "You're a very, very lucky little slave. I want to see what you're worth. Are you worth my time? Are you even able to serve properly? Who trained you? Scrub my fucking loo, you waste of space."

Of course, I left the toilet unflushed after I went, just a little gift. But I was flirting, I guess, being nice. Afterward, I told him to leave without saying a word. He returned to Jezebella a month later, buying more leather goods and jewelry, but I never granted him another session.

The entire encounter lasted maybe twenty minutes. I made $150 while running my shop. He got precisely what he needed; whatever psychological itch required scratching that particular afternoon. I was good at this. The dominance. The coldness. The control. Which is ironic, considering the absolute chaos that surrounded my business partnership with Ashley, a woman who had zero control over anything in her life, least of all herself.

She hadn't had a real relationship since the father of her son got 9 years for armed robbery at Citibank on 23rd and 6th Avenue. We were both summoned to the DA's office downtown, where we identified her moronic ex, who was, in fact, the same guy caught on surveillance camera in Citibank with a fake bomb! I simply couldn't get enough of this story as it was unfolding. Bryan, Ashley's baby daddy, attempted to board a mass transit city bus after robbing a bank. But when the bus driver wouldn't break the hundred-dollar bill he'd pulled from the stolen cash in his backpack, he was forced to get off the bus. This far-fetched and incredible series of events evidently led the authorities on an extremely pathetic trip straight to his apartment he shared with Ashley. A paltry three grand was found under the bed, you know, the one with the party dresses hanging around it. So, he was sentenced to serve his bid upstate, at Fishkill. That was Ashley's baby daddy, a real winner, but he did possess the essential blue eyes that made him irresistible to Ashley.

Early on, these tales were precisely why I had found Ashley so intriguing. She didn't appear interested in a mate or partner, and I hadn't yet met a man who truly wanted to date Ashley, or possessed the necessary tools to deal with her.

Well, there was this whole drama involving the superintendent of the building where Jezebella was located on 7th Street. Louis, a fat, thirty-five-year-old crackhead from Puerto Rico, happened to have blue eyes. For Ashley, that was enough! She threw herself at him, manipulating the poor slob into getting a tattoo of her image, with her name placed over his heart. She found it absolutely hilarious to convince these clueless men to engrave her portrait onto their chests, then promptly dump them. It was one of the things that amused her to no end. She'd counted three men whom she'd convinced to have her image etched onto their chests. I thought it a weird necessity, and ultimately, it was just to humiliate some unsuspecting man she'd met, for no apparent reason.

I discovered Louis, the building's superintendent, had been stealing from the store while Larry tended to it, and had also squeezed Crazy Glue into the shop's front door keyhole. All because of his infatuation with Ashley, who no doubt was feeding him some crazed lies to make him suddenly change from a seemingly regular, lazy, crackhead building super, to a diabolical, thieving, glue-crazed menace. Ashley was infectious to those who were unaware.

So, I called in a locksmith to change the locks after the Crazy Glue incident. I knew it was him, and he might have even copped to the fact he did it. Ashley was the first white blond woman who'd shown any interest in this out-of-shape, soon-to-be-unemployed meat-head. The whole mess culminated in me having to hire some thugs to "sort him out" after he tried robbing the shop, another mess she had been the cause of, which should probably concern me more than it does.

Ashley's chaos was exhausting. Every interaction with her involved some level of manipulation, theft, or manufactured crisis. Which made clients like Jimmy Tickles all the more remarkable by contrast. I must mention this client because he really stood out. Jimmy was the antithesis of chaos. Jimmy was reliable, sweet, and surprisingly talented.

Jimmy was a thirty-something-year-old assistant pharmacist who lived with his mother in Staten Island. I know what you're thinking, but no, he never got me any pills, not that I hadn't considered asking him. We called Jimmy "Tickles," because of his fetish. Jimmy would book me for two or three hours every week, and then proceed to tickle me. Non-stop. Yes, just tickle me. I hated it, but I really liked the big tip. He never wanted to be touched or masturbate. And although Jimmy did possess a rather large penis, he never had sex with any of us women. He just wanted to go down on me, after tickling me to near death.

The odd and uncomfortable thing about tickling, I discovered, is that I tended to lose sensitivity after about five minutes. And from there on, I would have to fake my hysterical screams and fits of giggles. He loved my theatrics, and I wanted to make him happy. I always want my clients to be happy with the service I provide.

Jimmy's short, terribly unhygienic, greasy, yet awfully sweet, and he had a talent. One I've never, ever encountered in another human. He could make a woman cum in twenty seconds, and under! I kid you not. He's famous around the whorehouses I worked in. And is the only man I've ever met who's acquired this talent. Plus, he always left a large, highly appreciated tip. That's a talent developed when you've grown up hanging around hookers, paying for sex, and actually taking notes.

Most men will never acquire this. Most men think porn has taught them everything they need to know about women's bodies. Jimmy knew better. Jimmy had done his homework.

I learned to move between these extremes without thinking. To be hard when hardness was required, to be open and kind when it served. To dominate and to submit, to teach and to perform, to feel nothing and sometimes, despite my best efforts, to feel something real.

The slave in my shop and Jimmy Tickles would never meet, would never know the other existed. But they're connected in my memory, two points on a spectrum so wide most people can't imagine it exists. Between them lies every variation of human need, dysfunction, loneliness, and desire you can conceive of. And probably a dozen more you can't.

THE BLOOD-STAINED BED

"Prostitution is the only job where the boss is also the criminal."— *Margot St. James*

I had been living at the Hotel Chelsea for about a month, in Room 102. It was the only available larger one-bedroom apartment with a huge living room and kitchen that Mr. Bard had shown me. I promptly arranged for the doctor to put a deposit on my new home.

The Hotel Chelsea appeared to be furnished with people's long-lost possessions, rearranged into various other rooms. I found the furnishings charming and perfectly eccentric. They fit me wholly. The mismatched furniture told stories of former residents who had left pieces of their lives behind, creating an atmosphere that felt oddly comforting.

With my few possessions (art from Stephen Sprouse, my Vivienne Westwood clothing collection, and my cat, Iggy) I moved right in with just a suitcase and a box of books. The transition felt seamless, as if the hotel had been waiting for me all along.

I clawed into consciousness around noon. Needless to say, I wasn't a morning person. My idea of a perfect morning was night. But never mind that.

I felt my beautiful Maine Coon cat, Iggy, jump on the bed, rubbing his nose in my hair, purring loudly and telling me it was time for breakfast.

I rolled onto my side to pet him, and as I did, I noticed the fitted bottom sheet had pulled from the corner of the bed, revealing a kind of muddy color underneath.

My interest now heightened, I had to get out of bed to investigate further. I slowly peeled back the sheet to see what was beneath... And I gasped, my hand flying to my mouth! I was stunned. Underneath the sheet, on the bed in which I had been sleeping (if you can call it that) for the past month, was a cluster of massive, wavy rings in various shades of brown. The patterns spread across the mattress like some grotesque abstract painting, each ring telling its own dark story.

Now, I had never seen this much blood, dried or otherwise, but blood it most definitely was: old, brown human seepage. But whose could it be... Oh, no!

This clearly wasn't some nosebleed or, to put it daintily, a menstrual mishap. No, what I was staring at was the site of a full-on, bad-news, story-at-eleven, monstrous bleed-out, and quite possibly death. And not by natural causes. The sheer volume of blood suggested something far more sinister than any accident could account for.

I stood back, shocked. Iggy jumped back onto the bed, eagerly sniffing at this abstract stain caused by human suffering. Something certain artists insist upon to create their most powerful works. But this mattress could and would be classified as art today, wouldn't it? Morbid art, perhaps, but art nonetheless. But I'm getting off track.

How far did this "pattern" seep? I had to look underneath to investigate. Wouldn't you? It's not easy moving a big, old, dusty mattress, but fueled by morbid curiosity, I managed to raise one side just enough to view the box spring. And, friends, let me tell you, it wasn't good. There's no other term for it; it was horrific.

The stain, you see, had leaked through the entire king-sized mattress and soaked through to the box spring below. To say I was stunned is putting it mildly; it was beyond revolting. The blood had penetrated so deeply that it had become part of the bed's very structure, a permanent testament to whatever had occurred here.

For a few moments, I just stood there, contemplating the magnitude of blood that had not so much splattered as oozed. The slow, deliberate way it had spread suggested someone had lain there for quite some time, their life essence gradually seeping into the fabric of the hotel itself.

Somebody (I assumed it was human, but who knows) appeared to have been left to drip and ooze and bleed out. The thought sent a chill through me, yet I found myself strangely fascinated by the macabre discovery.

My mind immediately wandered back to the infamous narrative about Room 100. It was an unavoidable tale if you were an eleven-year-old British kid with a rebellious interest in Anarchy and the newly emerging Punk scene. Sid Vicious had been charged with stabbing his girlfriend, Nancy Spungen, in Room 100. But this was Room 102, so it couldn't be, could it? The coincidence seemed too perfect, too horrifically poetic.

The thing about addiction is, nothing else matters. Sleeping on a biohazard nest dyed in blood might make some of you queasy. Me? Well, I'm not proud to say it, but I went about my day as usual. You know: wake up, get well, bank, taxi, cop, get high, taxi, home, get high, repeat. The routine had become so automatic that even discovering I had been sleeping in what amounted to a crime scene couldn't break the cycle.

Plus, I had developed a nasty bit of cocaine psychosis, which had taken over my ability to function rationally. I could probably have been diagnosed at that time as schizophrenic. So, any form of logical thinking was something I had trouble with, and had ever since I began speedballing. The drugs had rewired my brain in ways that made the abnormal seem perfectly acceptable.

I don't know anyone who gets high like I do (you know, the vast quantity of uppers and downers, mixed with alcohol and pills, and the needles) so I had isolated myself in the bathroom. I only saw people who could support my habits and lifestyle. I was confused, lonely, and racing through the years; I had always been racing to the finish line, though I was never quite sure what that finish line represented.

Then I ran into Jerome. Let me introduce the old (maybe 60, but some of those OGs look 25 years older than their age), rail-thin handyman who fed, Iggy, when I was away. Jerome was one of those fixtures of the Chelsea, a man who had seen everything and somehow managed to keep functioning despite it all.

Jerome shuffled around the hotel, fixing odds and ends. Often, he was mopping up busted pipes and human discharge. You know, vomit, blood, and clogged toilets. The man had become immune to the horrors that most people would find unbearable. We had become friendly, and I felt he would be the right man to ask about my newly discovered stained mattress.

It was during the quiet hours, when the rest of the world was asleep, that my only companion, psychosis, returned to feast upon my fragile brain again. The walls would whisper secrets, and shadows would dance in ways that defied physics.

You see, I had spent speedball-fueled 3 am walks around the hotel. I would glide over the beautiful old tiled floors in my red velvet slippers, wandering throughout the musty halls of the Chelsea, searching for the famous Room 100. But I could never find it.

The hotel seemed to shift and change during those late-night explorations through the corridors leading to dead ends that hadn't been there the day before.

And so, it seemed like a perfect opportunity to ask the one human who knew more than anyone on earth about the hotel: the old handyman.

Jerome looked me dead in the eye and, with his undecipherable drawl, said, "Room 100? ... Oh, my Oh my." He shook his head, staring at the ground. He didn't want to tell me anything, as if speaking about it might conjure something better left undisturbed. "Why don't you go down and find Mr. Stanley? He'll know... he'll know."

Aiming a wink and a nod of the head my way, Jerome moved his bucket and mop out of the elevator. "You be careful now, miss."

Was that a warning? Were dangers lurking around the corners in this building? Of course, there are.

So, fast forward to later that week. I saw Stanley Bard, the proprietor of the hotel, who actually ran the place and could usually be found in the lobby area or behind the front desk. Stanley was a legend in his own right, a man who had presided over decades of artistic chaos and drama and death.

You can see, there was no pressing need to discover what I was actually resting my body upon nightly, because that's what chronic drug abuse will do to you. It makes anything else in your life inconsequential. Even the childhood abuse memories were temporarily forgotten by my dulled mind. The drugs created a buffer between me and reality that made sleeping on a blood-soaked mattress seem like just another quirky detail of hotel living.

"Ah, Stanley, nice day, huh? So good to see you. I've a question that perhaps you might help me with."

"Hello, dear." He smiled, taking off his bifocal glasses and letting them hang around his neck, the New York Post folded under his armpit.

I explained as tactfully as possible, trying to find the right words for such an unusual complaint.

"Well, I've been here about a month now... and the other morning I noticed that there's a rather large, um... brown, kind of color of dried blood, very old dried blood, covering the majority of the mattress, and, uh, you know since I'm sleeping on it and all, I thought maybe um it was a little gross and could I get a different mattress? I mean if it's not a problem..."

My voice trailed off, and I saw Stanley scrutinizing me, searching my face for any sign I was kidding around. And I wasn't. I was deadly serious, though I realized how surreal the conversation must have sounded.

"Remind me what room you're in, dear?"

"Room 102."

"Ah, Room 102. Well, that used to be Room 100.

We just changed the numbers around and made two rooms into one suite, to keep the tourists and sickos from comin' around. They'd leave empty bottles of Jack Daniels, fan mail, and upside-down crosses outside the door. But it's the animal remains and satanic shit that got out of hand, and it was becoming a problem. So, I came up with the plan to lose Room 100 to the past. We now jump straight to 102. It's like it never happened."

He smiled, putting his glasses back on, as if this simple numerical sleight of hand could erase history.

"Yes, and about that... the remains of Room 100 most definitely have remained, pardon the pun... and, um, do you want to come and see what I've discovered?" I offered.

"Oh dear! No, not necessary, I'm extremely sorry... I, I, I had no idea! I can't believe they didn't remove the bed after that unfortunate circumstance. It was a difficult month. I thought someone was taking care of that mess." He drifted off, lost in memories of that hectic time when the hotel had been thrust into the international spotlight for all the wrong reasons.

Stanley Bard, the inveterate New Yorker, just stared at me, perhaps calculating the liability of having left a guest sleeping on what amounted to evidence from a crime scene.

"Can't do everything myself, can I?" He fumbled with his New York Post newspaper in his hands, glancing at the headlines as if seeking refuge in the day's ordinary disasters.

"No," I managed. "You certainly can't do everything. It must have been overlooked, totally understandable how a bloodied mattress can be left in a hotel room after a highly publicized murder. You had other things to contend with." I said, trying not to, God forbid, embarrass him, but in awe at his excuse. The casual way he dismissed such a monumental oversight was almost as shocking as the discovery itself.

"Exactly. So glad you understand what I'm dealing with. If only my other guests were as understanding as you. I'll have it taken care of, dear, and get you a brand-new mattress right away." He half-smiled, patting my hand with the practiced gesture of a man who had spent decades managing the impossible.

The eternal well-mannered Brit and my manners kicked in. I was practically apologizing, like it was my bloody blood that had soaked through to the box springs. The absurdity of the situation (me feeling guilty for complaining about sleeping on a murder scene) would have been laughable if it weren't so perfectly representative of how addiction had warped my sense of normal.

And with that, I turned and went back upstairs to my Room 102, carrying with me the knowledge that I had been sleeping in the very spot where Nancy Spungen had met her violent end.

The discovery added another layer to my already complex relationship with the Chelsea. Here was a place where art and death intermingled, where the boundaries between creativity and destruction blurred beyond recognition. I was living in a monument to punk rock tragedy, sleeping in the physical remnants of a love story gone horribly wrong.

In the days that followed, I found myself studying the stains with a kind of morbid fascination. Each ring and discoloration told part of Nancy's story. Her final moments played out in brown and rust-colored patterns across the mattress. It was grotesque and beautiful in equal measure, a piece of accidental art created by the most tragic of circumstances.

The fact that I continued to sleep there night after night spoke to how completely drugs had rewired my priorities. What should have been horrifying had become just another detail in my daily existence.

The blood-stained bed became a metaphor for my entire life at that point: sleeping peacefully atop the evidence of destruction, cushioned by chemicals from the reality of what lay beneath.

P.S. They never came to change the mattress, so I continued to sleep in a biohazard nest. Stanley's promise, , simply evaporated into the ether of good intentions never acted upon.

THE NIGHT I DIED IN THE HOTEL CHELSEA

"Quite simply I was in love with New York. I do not mean "love" in any colloquial way...you'll never love anyone quite that way again.' — Joan Didion

There was no climax, no warning, no moment of grace. Just the slow erosion of whatever light I once had. I didn't fall off a cliff; I dissolved, one hit at a time, until there was barely enough left of me to die. When death finally came for me, it took me peacefully, willingly. Because this is what it really looks like when the end begins.

On a shelf in the bathroom of my room, I set up my hit. Spoon, works, lighter, coke and dope.

I threw two bags of dope into the caked spoon and a nice big hit of coke. I deserved it. I wanted to hear the bells ringing in my ears and the fantastic rush good cocaine delivers when injected I.V. I tied off my right arm with a shoelace I kept around my neck and found a vein unusually quickly. I drew up the blood, and with a sigh that echoed off the walls, pressed down the plunger fast, feeling my soul uncoil.

The rush. Then that familiar life-saving warmth of heroin. I tasted it at the back of my throat and settled into that momentary blissful suspended comfort, like a warm candle-lit bath or a tight bear hug from someone who cares.

Seconds later, BAM! Coke shot up to my brain, exploding behind my eyeballs. My heart thumped through my ribs as ecstasy flooded my body. I cupped my ears with my hands, struggling to shut out the loud ringing bells in my brain. How could I still see with my eyes shut? Everything blurred, and I prayed to God to slow my heart. I immediately knew I had done too much coke, but unfortunately there's nothing you can do to reverse a hit of cocaine after the fact. I grabbed the edge of the sink, supporting myself, and caught a fleeting glimpse in the mirror: scared, dark eyes ringed in smudged black mascara, swollen pupils. My heart, it hurts... "Breathe... breathe... slowly," I whispered, but I knew it was too much. Take me, fuck it, take me... I can't hold on. I couldn't feel my limbs. I clenched and unclenched my fists, trying to sense my body, struggling with all my might not to fall to the floor. I couldn't hold on, I was going... going down.

And the floor came up to meet my head.

As I fell, I slipped into a tunnel and began to travel swiftly through it. I was dead.

I viewed the scene in the bathroom from above. Random faces that I had known throughout my life were on the sidelines, watching me, waving, looking at me, judging me. I sped past them, touching their fingers as they waved. And yes, at the very end of the tunnel, I saw a light. It appeared, at first, as no more than a distant pinprick. Then it began to glow, a warm, comforting light that somehow beckoned me, that pulled me slowly closer. But still... it was so very far away. I knew as sure as I had known anything that I must get to the blissful comforting glow. This light, in ways I could not yet comprehend, was my destiny, my calling, my everything.

The light, I now understood, was my resting place. And it wanted me. It felt so warm, so loving. A comfort I had never experienced. And so, I gave in. I drifted blissfully towards this wondrous illumination. This gift I had, without knowing, so badly needed.

And then suddenly, and rudely, I must add, I was jolted back out of the perfect bliss, thrust from nirvana, back to this familiar dark realm. Back to the cold, back to the pain, back to the screaming darkness, back to God no, please, not this, back to the horror. Back to LIFE! I sensed the bed beneath my body. I was no longer in the bathroom, and someone whose voice I recognized as the Doctor, was beside me. The man who paid my bills and bought me bags of Valium, the man who filled my bank account with $10K a month just for expenses, which were essentially drugs.

"Hey there... Zoe, hi," he said, in that unflappable way he has of talking. Maybe it was the doctor in him. "I see you're back..." he whispered. I felt his hand on my arm, and I opened my eyes, and nothing. I saw only darkness, blackness. I was blind! I'll say it again. I opened my eyes and I was blind. Try to imagine.

What would you do?

Immediately, a fear and horror I had never known filled the pit of my stomach and drenched my entire being in sweat. I closed my eyes and opened them, again and again. And I couldn't see anything. Zilch.

I panicked. Frantically, I grabbed for the doctor's arm. "Oh my God," I blubbered,

"I can't see...I can't see anything...!"

Cocaine still racing through my system, amplifying the terror and paranoia a thousand times, I began to sob. And I sobbed like a child. But I am an emotional child. I pulled the covers over my head, and there I lay, waiting and praying to die. Take me, Goddess, I'm begging you. I can't live this life any longer. I've destroyed myself.

I couldn't comprehend what I had done. I hated myself. I hated this... But what was "this?" I sniveled. I wailed, my words half-garbled and charged with pain. If I had a mother, I would cry for her. If I had a father, I would cry for him. But I'm alone. And so, I bawled for myself. For the life I lost. The children I might have had, friends I would never meet, art I would never make, and a book I would never complete. It was over, and my life was gone.

All I could do was lie here on the stinking, blood-stained bed that had stolen another life. How many lives had this room swallowed?

I obsessed over how I had finally gone and done it. I had wrecked my life. I had, through my own recklessness, my own desperation, my pain, blinded myself. I had tried so hard with narcotics to escape, yet to understand how to live in this world, and now instead, I was trapped. How will I live? How will I be able to do anything?

For good measure, The Doctor told me my heart had stopped; I had been dead for a total of three minutes! I wondered why he didn't call an ambulance. But I guess, because he's a doctor, he didn't think it was necessary. I didn't understand. But then, at this point, I didn't understand much of anything. And I was in no position to argue. So, there I lay, pondering my god-awful waste of a life.

The thing is, I had shown so much promise. Even five years ago, I had the beginning of what could have been an actual career in the fashion and art world. Then life got in the way.

I prayed to the God I'd been brought up with and the Goddess to whom I am now devoted. I prayed for my sight to be regained. I made all the futile and familiar promises addicts make when we're in a corner. I would do anything, if I could just open my eyes... and see.

With cocaine rushing through my system, my mind was falling into the dreams and hallucinations created by the life-killing quantity of drugs in my blood. This wasn't my first OD, but it was perhaps the most memorable.

Do you want to know what happened next? You've come this far. Well, something I can only describe as miraculous. After what could have been a day, or a minute, but was actually about six hours, I began to see wavy outlines of the old wooden dresser I had spray-painted silver with my best friend Brian.

Then the dim light overhead began to brighten, and I could make out a stream of sunlight blasting through the shuttered windows. Tears flowing down my face, I collapsed into nothing less than total relief. You can't tell me I don't have ancestors and spiritual guides taking care of me.

You know what I'm thinking, right? You should know me well by now. You'd think maybe, just maybe, I'd learned something, but addiction isn't about learning; it's an all-encompassing illness that won't settle until it has destroyed you and everything you thought you were.

I gathered all my strength and peeled myself off the bed. I walked unsteadily to the living room, grabbing walls and furniture to steady me.

The room looked the same as it had before, I died. "Where's my dope?" I asked the Doctor, frantically searching surfaces. "Where is it, where did you hide it?" I cried.

What about my prayers and promises? All the pleading to the Goddess! I had begged and bargained for my sight to return. And now that it has, all my pledges are forgotten and gone. How abysmal, what a disgrace. I am so mortified at who I've become.

I've dropped out of existence; none of my old friends know where I am. I'm only a few blocks away, but I've barricaded myself into the bathroom in old Room 100, which I rarely leave.

The world continues to spin as my mind struggles to grasp reality. I don't know who is the president; I don't know the day of the week. I have no comprehension of anything; my brain has been changed, and I live in a world I've created, in my room at the Hotel. Like so many artists before me, I've been lured to this glorious building, enticed and manipulated by the lost souls who roam the halls and stand in the shadows in empty rooms, observing us in this realm.

I wish I could say I learned my lesson. But listen: it's not about learning anything, it's about killing the pain. So please, do not be alarmed when I tell you that the first thing I did once my vision returned was go straight to the cooker and slam another hit.

A CROAKER'S WAITING ROOM

"One must be a bit wild, a bit dangerous to be truly alive". — "I was determined to live not merely exist"
— Colette

I came back from the dead, but not from my addiction. The light faded, the shadows moved back in, and so did I, straight to the cooker like nothing had happened. I'd prayed and made all the useless promises one makes when you're in that position. A promise is whispered when you think you're dying. When I could see again, I saw only one thing: the next hit. And if I was going to keep breathing, I'd need more than luck. I'd need a script. A clean, white, government-sanctioned, insurance-defrauding little piece of paper. So, I dug up an old phone number a friend had offered. "When you're in need, call this number." It led all the way to an old croaker's office, because when death fails, bureaucracy steps in.

I don't expect many readers to know what a "croaker doctor" is, so I'll explain. Very simply, a croaker is an old slang term used to describe a medical doctor. I first heard the term from William Burroughs in his memoir Junky. The term has been adapted in certain circles to describe an older gentleman doctor who writes prescriptions that most doctors won't, or can't legally write.

I know things have changed mightily over the past few decades, but this was still a time when, occasionally, you could locate a "dodgy" medical doctor who could set you up with Morphine, Demerol, Methadone, speed. You know, the good stuff. Generally benefiting from word-of-mouth advertising, you might be able to form a picture of who these gracious doctors attract.

Naturally, I called the number promptly and was told through a taped recording to come to 11th Street and Broadway, Suite 312. Hours were from 9 AM to 1 PM. The office charge was $50 (cash!), which was emphasized. First come, first served. That's all the instructions I was given, and needed.

When I arrived at Suite 312 at ten to nine, there were three people ahead of me who stared at the floor and fidgeted. Within five minutes, an impressive line of runny-nosed patients, bums and executives alike, were lining down the hall and stairs. I thanked God I had set my alarm!

Then movement. After what seemed like a never-ending ten minutes, the door was unlocked, and a head peeked out. Appearing like Oz from behind a heavy green door, Doctor Grave's morning greeting seemed more of a grimace than a smile. But I'll get into that in a minute. He was the professional, and I was surmising he knew his clientele didn't care much for the bedside manner that most patients usually insist upon.

The doctor left the waiting room door open. I gathered we were to follow along while he disappeared again behind another door. Five minutes later, the first patient was called as the good doctor yelled "Next!" I inched up a foot. Now that progress was being made, some of the patients made small talk. We aren't the chattiest bunch in the early morning.

The first patient was seen and out the door within three minutes! We, the eagerly awaiting patients, sat knee to knee along a couch, eyes nervously all on the large green door where the great doctor, or Oz as I jokingly referred to him, ruled from.

A dusty Art Deco mahogany wardrobe had been pushed against a wall and unfortunately seemed forgotten. In the corner were piles of papers and files that had fallen and scattered, appearing to have been stepped on, judging by the heavy footprints. Was that gold foil wallpaper? A tad worn, but gorgeous nonetheless, and it must have been from a few long decades ago. Over two long 1980s farmhouse-style couches hung a timeworn, slightly wonky print of a British fox hunt in a gold frame.

Unless you've been in a detox ward or an old person's assisted living home, you might not be aware of these particular country-farm couch designs from hell. These couches are made to withstand time, and the synthetic material is rough and nubbly. The whole couch is a dirt magnet, and the plaid print hides clumsy stains and the leakage that sick humans' ooze. I have spent some time in hospitals during the 1990s for these couches to trigger me so.

Anyway, they were likely designed for the institution community and probably made for a buck a day by the locked-up institution community themselves. America is working the throw-away people for whatever they have left in them. Toss them a dollar and tell them to be grateful. At least they are employed today, behind bars.

Now, I don't want to appear judgmental, but who amongst us hasn't judged? We all do it. But I'm going to say it: this clientele looked really sketchy. Not that a little sketch ever bothered me, absolutely not. But how on earth did the good doctor get away with doing this? My curiosity peaked. I mean, this was hardly covert, clandestine meetings.

No, this was an old office building (a century ago, it was a beautiful hotel) that housed multiple mental health professionals, along with, coincidentally, an old literary agent of mine, and other thoroughly respectable, non-criminal operations under this one roof. With every minute, the waiting room got busier. People seemed to know one another and managed a respectable "Good morning" nod. I eagerly awaited my turn as the person in front of me came dashing out of the doctor's office in two short minutes with his script in hand.

I heard a rather gruffly yelled "NEXT!" I jumped up and walked into the other room to meet the good doctor. Who needs a receptionist when you can yell NEXT!"?

I beamed a pleasant grin and reached my hand out over the piles of paper and files stacked upon his desk. He inched his buttocks forward in his chair, seemingly annoyed to have to stretch his arm out, and softly finger-shook my hand.

This was the first time I'd gotten a good look at Doctor Grave, and I couldn't take my eyes off his face. I was looking in wonder at his extremely tight, wrinkle-free, smooth-as-a-baby's-butt-cheek skin. Did I say milky? It was extraordinary. His whole face was pulled and pinched upwards, lifting any sagging jowls to the Gods. With light breaking through the dusty windows, I was now aware of his incredible blue eyeballs. He'd added a nice dollop of clear mascara upon his lashes. Frankly, I appreciated the effort.

"I had a face lift, what do you think?" Doctor Grave asked, holding up his chin, giving his best "Voguing" profile, framing his face with his thumb and index finger.

"Oh, I think you look fabulous, I'd never have known," I exclaimed.

I'm always delighted to be in the company of gays. Those are my people. But did he ask every patient what they thought of his new face? How bizarre.

"Do you really?" He looked me up and down, giving me the once-over, and bestowed an approving wink and a pouty half-smile. "I had my eyes done six months ago, and everyone says I just look so rested, and that no one can tell. They say I look twenty-five years younger! Isn't that marvelous?" he enthusiastically exclaimed.

Hearing how excited Doctor Grave (and I did love his name) became after discussing his face, I took no time in complimenting him on his style and oh-so-youthful glow. Truth was, Doctor Grave was bizarre looking. His refreshed, younger eyes had left him with a permanent surprised look, and his left eye appeared a bit droopy, but it added so much character.

Doctor Grave liked me, mainly because I'm certain I was the only patient who'd had time for a morning tête-à-tête,, and I doubted anyone had taken a moment to really talk, as in converse, or maybe just listen to him, in decades.

Once in Grave's actual office, I was even more surprised. It was as dark as the waiting room, yet stuffier if that's possible. There was nothing that resembled a doctor's office. No instruments to take blood pressure, no jars of wooden-tongue depressors, no thermometer. What, no eye chart!?

Grave sat behind his gigantic heavy antique desk, buried beneath a mountain of papers that he'd forgotten about long ago. In fact, I'd bet hard money that he slept in that old desk chair on many a lonely night. There were two chairs meant for patients, and I moved a few papers over a little so I could nudge my bum onto the dusty flattened cushion.

"So, what do you want?" There was that surly, annoyed tone again, which wouldn't deter me one bit from getting what I came here for.

"So, yes, um, Doctor, I wanted to perhaps ask you for some, um, Methadone, if possible," I said, crossing my fingers, pressing them into my lap with a fixed pleasant smile upon my face.

I waited for him to give me that suspicious glare and stand up and sternly order me from the premises. But he said nothing. I think he was looking for his prescription pad. So, I added a little lie just for conversation's sake while he searched his desk.

"It's for a trip I am taking in a week, you know, work...." I nervously rambled. Work. Why did I say that? Now he's going to assume I'm a working person and ask for insurance, which I obviously don't have. Oh well, heck, better try and see if I can get some Valiums.

"Oh, and doctor, while you're at it, maybe toss in thirty Valiums. I've got a terrible insomnia issue at the moment, and only Valiums help, not those Halcyons that some doctor gave me last time. Terrible bit of business, those things had me all messed up. Do sleeping pills make you sleepwalk? Oh, and doctor, if you could add twenty...five or so Morphine pills, that would be ever so helpful. Back pain from a gym injury, the pain never leaves me. I'm really extremely healthy..." I trailed off.

If he thought I went to the gym, surely, he'd assume I'm not an addict, just a nice lady who goes to the gym. I definitely was having a grand old-time storytelling this morning.

"Doctor, I think I need the name of your surgeon, you look like a teenager, close up!" I smiled up at his stretched, smooth, pinkish skin and added, "I just can't believe you're over 35 years old." I beamed my best Cheshire cat grin.

If you thought I was pushing it by adding Valiums and Morphine, already on top of the trusted Methadone, you'd be right. Another more scrupulous doctor might have seen the red flags waving wildly in the dark, musty office and, for the benefit of myself and mankind, declined my request as "dangerous." But Grave was special, as the winding patient line suggested. Listening to my praise of his new face, he just couldn't resist giving me exactly what I requested.

He looked at me as though we were long-lost

siblings.

"It's incredible, isn't it? Oh, honey, you're just so kind. What is it you say you do, dear?"

"Oh, I'm a writer." I smiled.

"Oh yeah, what do you write? Like magazines and stuff? You know I read all the men's magazines, mainly I like the articles in Esquire and Details. But honey, while at the check-out at D'Agostino's, I can't put the Enquirer down! Did you see Aliens are on Earth, but refuse to wear clothing!? And they know where Elvis has been hiding! I knew he was alive. Do you write for one of those magazines, dear?"

"Oh, I wish, that's my idea of a dream job. Back when I was in the fashion business, I worked as a stylist and make-up artist for a large number of editorial spreads. It was long ago when I was young and the new girl on the scene in New York. Now I'm writing a memoir."

"Oh, how marvelous. Well, you'll have to drop off a copy of your book, won't you? I have some esteemed patients." He leaned in closely. "Some very famous people come to see me... you know, when they are in town, of course." He winked and looked directly into my eyes, as though conveying an unspoken knowledge and understanding we had between us.

"Of course," I nodded, picturing some skinny alternative musician, dope fiend, thumbing through his little black address book. Searching for that number someone passed him a year ago, adding, "If ever in need, and in New York City, and want a little something, call this phone number: 352-7891. Doctor Grave."

I knew this wasn't the type of place where the doctor treats or cures anyone. I mean, sure, he's certainly helping us, and at that moment he was Oz. He was the holy one who made addicts wait for undisclosed amounts of time before writing a prescription for narcotics reserved for the dying.

But we were all sorta dying. I mean, hopefully not today, but one day. Besides, it doesn't take a degree to understand that this doctor was perhaps adding to the deeply narcotic-addicted America. I'd go so far as to say maybe Doctor Grave had a little chippy of his own. As long as he continues to write, patients will continue to fork over the $50 or so for a three-minute visit.

I like to talk, and never have I found one person that I can't find something to spitball about. I also like oddballs, the stranger the better, and Grave was something of a distinctive character.

As we both chatted, forgetting about time, I sensed the heat from the other side of the door. The door that led to the waiting room, which by now, some forty-five minutes later, was probably filled to the breaking point of some wildly pissed-off, sweating junkies. "I'll never get out of here alive!" Surely, they were all plotting on how to kill me.

I handed Doctor Grave his $50 charge. He told me to please come by anytime and repeated "anytime," and I saw a wistful loneliness in his new eyes that lingered with me. Maybe I will go back and see him, just to see how he's doing.

I took a deep breath and swung open the heavy door to a stuffy waiting room of spitting glares. They had no idea who I was or who I thought I was. I strolled through the room of sick, tired, and waiting bodies, feeling their eyes shredding me. I smiled ever so slightly as I felt for the scripts in my pocket.

Epilogue

For forty years, chaos was my home. I chased oblivion through heroin, cocaine, pills, and alcohol. Anything that could quiet the screaming pain inside me for a few hours. I believed I was beyond saving, that I'd crossed an invisible line with no way back. Eventually, I broke. I surrendered. Time for a different kind of silence, in a different town, far far away.

The New York I loved for forty years had become a ghost town made of memories. I could no longer survive inside it.

It still surprises me I outlived so many of my friends. Eight years ago, after a long relapse, a collapsed abusive marriage, and a suicide attempt, I landed in the locked ward at Gracie Square Hospital. Beige walls, and heavy doors with no door handles, so we don't try to hang ourselves. For ten days I listened to people scream into the void, wondering if this was rock bottom or if lower levels await.

When they finally released me, my boyfriend, soon to be my husband, put me on a plane to Los Angeles. I knew nothing about LA. It felt foreign and exposed, and so awfully sunny after New York's shadowy avenues. I quit every substance and began to see and breathe for the first time, that I can remember.

My son is my everything and we speak daily. Our connection is so ancient, cellular, older than reason. He keeps me alive and present. Watching him grow into the strong, remarkable man he has become is my greatest reward. It is why I am still here.

Thirty years ago, after reading Jerry's first memoir, I realized he was my guy. I knew I'd just have to wait to meet him. Some truths arrive early and wait patiently for the rest of your life to catch up. Years later, after marrying him, the man I knew I would wait to find, I turned my life around completely. Jerry's unconditional love did save me, and he gave me significantly more. We are meant to be together, and I've never been more content or happier.

Prostitution was not my tragedy. It was my initiation. A hard education. A place where illusion was reality and survival demanded precision. Sex work taught me boundaries, intuition, and how to read people in seconds. It forced me to understand power, loneliness, and vulnerability in ways most people never have to. I did not disappear there. I became sharper, stronger, smarter.

I lived on the edges in spaces the polite world pretends do not exist. Like the witches, the outcasts, the women who have always survived by instinct, I learned to move between worlds. My spiritual roots sank deep into Wicca, into the Goddess, and now Qigong. The body was never my enemy. It was my vessel. Survival is not a moment. It is a lifetime of learning how to stay.

I raised myself with no map and endless ways to fail. I lived in a world where performance and truth blurred, where survival meant becoming whoever I needed to be that day. I slept in drafty lofts and blood-stained beds. I watched people vanish. I learned how fragile life really is.

The streets were my real education. The sex workers I met were my professors, my sisters. They shaped me. They protected me.

This is not a redemption story.

It is not about forgiveness or grace.

It is about survival.

I did not outrun my past. I carried it with me and learned how to live anyway. I rewrote my own ending. I learned how to feel, how to remain alive long after the world had already decided I should not be.

The End

A true story. Some names have stayed the same and some changed to protect the guilty.

SPECIAL THANKS (no order)
Jerry Stahl, Lydia Lunch, Anne Hanavan, Jasmine Hirst, Puma Perl, Kimberly Biehl Boaz, Kim Dallesandro Diana Mahiques, Michael Alago, Robert Butcher, Danny Fields, Rachel Amodeo, Richard Edson, Johnathan Shaw, Meistorm Serpent, Michael Grodner, Johnny Stuntz, Chi Chi Valenti, Anne Cummings, Alex Kondracke, Ginger Coyote and Willie Crane at Far West Press.

IN MEMORY
Larry, The Doctor, Brian, Ashley.

RESPECT
86 street, GGs, 611, Monache Studios, All Manhattan, The Blue Velvet Club, Chrystie Street, Park Avenue, CPS, Hunts Point. This book is on behalf of all the people working the blade or track in their town & all the men and women who worked at Sterling Ladies and the Blue Velvet Club, thank you for your magick.

ALSO OUT ON FAR WEST

....

farwestpress.com

+1 (541) FAR-WEST

www.ingramcontent.com/pod-product-compliance
Lightning Source LLC
Chambersburg PA
CBHW031259130726
47988CB00007B/2641